THE WISE WOMAN

The Wise Woman

...how to be one in a thousand.

Joyce Rogers

MINISTRIES

MEMPHIS, TENNESSEE

Cover design: Julia Flanagan

First printing, 1980
Second printing, 1999

ISBN: 0-8054-5289-3
Dewey Decimal Classification: 248.843
Subject Headings: CHRISTIAN LIFE / / WOMEN
Library of Congress Catalog Card Number: 80-68538

Printed in the United States of America.

DEDICATION

This book is dedicated to my family. First of all to Mother and Daddy, who first loved me and introduced me to the things of the Lord. To my loving husband, whose courageous preaching of the Word of God has influenced and blessed my life more than has the preaching of any other person. To my two daughters, Gayle and Janice, who are like "cornerstones, polished after the similitude of a palace" (Psalm 144:12). To my two sons, Steve and David, who are like "plants, grown up in their youth" (Psalm 144:12).

ACKNOWLEDGMENTS

A special thanks to my daughter, Gayle, who typed and helped edit the manuscript and who greatly encouraged me. This book would not be a reality without her. Poems not attributed to another author are by Joyce Rogers. Poems by three of the author's children, Janice, Steve, and David, are also published in this volume.

Contents

INTRODUCTION

This book is not mere theory. It contains principles and illustrations tried in the crucible of real life. I suppose the greatest concept in living the Christian life is "balanced living." We are all tempted to get sidetracked on our own experience-oriented detours and place too much emphasis on one part or another of our Christian lives.

I believe with the "preacher" of Ecclesiastes that there is "a time to be born and a time to die...a time to weep and a time to laugh...a time to keep silence and a time to speak...." (Ecclesiastes 3:1, 4, 7). I hope that this balance is evidenced in these pages.

I believe that there should not be a definite division in the practical and the profound, the natural and the supernatural. As Oswald Chambers says, God's presence in our lives will make us "supernaturally natural and naturally supernatural."

Admittedly, this book is written from the perspective of a married woman. It is home- and family-centered because this has been the sphere to which God has called me to "work out" my salvation. That doesn't mean I think it is God's will for every woman to marry. God calls some to the high calling of singleness. I trust that even those who are single will find help and blessing in this book.

Join me now as we pursue the path of a wise woman.

Part I

A Wise Woman's Availability To God

CHAPTER ONE

THE SEARCH FOR A WISE WOMAN

—•—

> *I applied mine heart to know, and to search,*
> *and to seek out wisdom…Behold, this have I found,*
> *saith the preacher, counting one by one, to find out the account:*
> *Which yet my soul seeketh, but I find not:*
> *one man among a thousand have I found;*
> *but a woman among all those have I not found.*
> Ecclesiastes 7:25a, 27-28

What an indictment! The "preacher" of Ecclesiastes was on a treasure hunt, searching for a wise person. He could not find even "one woman in a thousand" who sought after wisdom.

As I read these words over and over again, I asked, "Lord, could you find one wise woman in a thousand today?" I know some women who would fit into this category, but they are far too few!

I wanted to be the kind of woman God could count on – a God-fearing woman, full of wisdom. I wanted to let God take control of my life, so to this end I prayed.

I'm Letting You

Today, and forever Lord
I'm letting You

Be God in me –
In action!

I'm bowing out and
I'm letting You bow in.
I'm going to let You
think through my mind
react through my emotions, and
make decisions through my will.

Here Lord, my body is available to You.
I've tried so many times
In my own strength
To be like You:

to copy
to imitate the good I saw in You.
But I'm finished with that now!

Come, take control of my life –
I want to be available, dear Jesus
to be what You want me to be
and do what You want me to do!

NATURAL WISDOM VS. GODLY WISDOM

What is wisdom? The dictionary defines it like this: "Knowledge practically applied to the best ends; natural sagacity; prudence; skill in affairs, piety."

People see wisdom as the ability to meet and evaluate the circumstances of life from their natural minds and experiences. This appears to be good, but it has many pitfalls.

Godly wisdom is what I so desperately need. Life is too complicated to try to figure things out from a human perspective. Only God's point of view is important. That is true wisdom.

"For My thoughts are not your thoughts, neither are your ways My ways," saith the LORD. For as the heavens are higher than the earth, so are My ways higher than your ways, and My thoughts than your thoughts. (Isaiah 55:8-9)

TIME AND JUDGMENT

Life is made up of both time and judgment. Every moment I must decide how I will use my time. Every day I must choose what is right.

Multitudes of projects clamor for my time. Some are good and some are bad. Some are in-between. There's not even time to do the good things much less the in-between things. I need more than my own natural wisdom to know *what* to do and *when* to do it.

As a woman of God I want to discern God's will. Nevertheless, life is sometimes confusing. There is a multitude of "good things" calling, "You can do it! You can do it! You can!" It is so difficult to decide what is best. One activity might be best at one time but not at another. Resting in the hammock might be best today, but wrong tomorrow. How can I possibly know where my priorities lie?

My mind is in constant demand to make judgments in other areas. Take this scenario:

Brother is watching the television. He walks out of the room. Sister comes in. She sees no one around and changes the channel. She is already absorbed in another show when Brother comes back into the room. He says, "I was here first!" Sister replies, "You left the room. I'm not changing the channel . . . Mother!"

Who is right and who is wrong in this scenario? Are both right and both wrong? How do I resolve the conflict?

How can I discover what I should do when family members are demanding my time and opinion? The phone is ringing; my lost neighbors are silently calling; the church is beckoning; and my community is begging me to respond to their needs. How I need wisdom far beyond my own! Ecclesiastes 8:5b-6a tells us, "A wise man's heart discerneth both time and judgment. Because to every purpose there is time and judgment."

A Hidden Treasure

> I applied mine heart to know, and to search, and to seek out wisdom. (Ecclesiastes 7:25)

How and where will I ever find the wisdom that I so desperately need? First, I must desire it with all my heart. Then, I must seek it diligently.

The Bible visualizes wisdom as a hidden treasure. I have a map to this treasure. It is God's Word! Join me in this search for the greatest treasure in the world – godly wisdom.

> My son, if thou wilt receive my words, and hide my commandments with thee; so that thou incline thine ear unto wisdom, and apply thine heart to understanding; Yea, if thou criest after knowledge, and liftest up thy voice for understanding; if thou seekest her as silver, and searchest for her as for hid treasures; then shalt thou understand the fear of the Lord, and find the knowledge of God. For the Lord giveth wisdom. (Proverbs 2:1-6a)

The Companions Of Wisdom

When I lay hold of wisdom, I will also find many side benefits. Most people constantly seek after happiness. They capture it for a brief moment, only to have it slip through their fingers. They wonder where it hides and how it can continually be theirs. The Bible says that when they find wisdom, they will stumble over happiness along the way.

> Happy is the man that findeth wisdom, and the man that getteth understanding. For the merchandise of it is better than the merchandise of silver, and the gain thereof than fine gold. She is more precious than rubies; and all the things thou canst desire are not to be compared unto her. Length of days is in her right hand; and in her left hand riches and honour. Her ways

are ways of pleasantness, and all her paths are peace. (Proverbs 3:13-18)

Long life will be in wisdom's right hand and riches and honor in her left. Along this path we will also meet two more of wisdom's companions – pleasantness and peace. Indeed these are the lasting treasures that my heart really longs for. Don't you agree that these treasures are worth more than silver, gold, or many precious jewels?

WHAT REALLY MAKES A WOMAN BEAUTIFUL?

A magazine caught my eye. On it was the picture of a striking woman. Underneath her picture was this provoking question: "What makes a woman beautiful?" I wanted to be beautiful so I read on. These items were listed: hairstyling, makeup, voice and diction, wardrobe, visual poise, social graces, personality development, and figure.

I agreed. All these factors are important in making a woman *outwardly* beautiful. I need all the help I can get in these areas. But as I pondered the list I became suddenly aware that something was missing. Not one thing was mentioned about "inner beauty," which is shown by wisdom, and how I could attain it.

I thought about my life and the lack of training I had in many of these areas. Then I paused. How eternally grateful I was for the training I had received – training to achieve "inner beauty."

My mother was inwardly beautiful. She challenged me in a quiet, unconscious way. She was a wise woman who was more interested in my making the "Lamb's Book of Life" than the social register.

Mother never taught me how to pour tea from a silver service, but she showed me the importance of the water of life. The spiritual side of life was always uppermost in her mind. Though she never attended a Bible school, she studied the Bible in-depth. She directed me to read many "inner beauty" research books written by some of the greatest Christians of all time.

To become *outwardly* beautiful I need expert counseling. I need to know what hairstyle is most becoming to me. I need to know what colors look best on me. I need to know what my flaws are and how I can compensate for them. I need to know how to magnify my good features. This advice is often very costly. Only the more well-to-do can afford the services of a beauty consultant or fashion expert. Those little do-it-yourself helps never seem to measure up to the professional help.

Inner beauty helps are quite the same. There are lot of do-it-yourself books, but they will never measure up to expert counseling. This professional help, however, is free of charge.

THE GREAT BEAUTY CONSULTANT

The Holy Spirit of God is the great beauty consultant. His beauty book is the Bible. It is fully illustrated with pictures of Jesus from Genesis to Revelation. The more you look at these pictures the more you will say, "Gladly I'll forfeit all of earth's treasures, Jesus, Thy perfect likeness to wear."[1]

You will be tempted to imitate, but you will discover that it is impossible to do it yourself. The Holy Spirit compares you to Jesus in order to make you dissatisfied with what you are. He knows that in your own strength the goal is impossible. Can you hear Him saying, "You cannot do it – but *I* can if you will just let me?" One of the chief facets of real beauty is simply God's wisdom shining through.

GOD'S UGLY SHOP

If a woman places her emphasis on outward beauty, she will be in a terrible mess. Someone has said, "Beauty is only skin deep, but ugly goes all the way to the bone. Beauty fades, but ugly holds her own." God has made an appointment in His "Ugly Shop" for those overly proud of their good looks. He will give a reverse treatment.

Such was the fate of the "haughty daughters of Zion." Read about it in Isaiah 3:16-26:

> Next, He will judge the haughty Jewish women, who mince along, noses in the air, tinkling bracelets on their ankles, with wanton eyes that rove among the crowds to catch the glances of the men. The Lord will send a plague of scabs to ornament their heads! He will expose their nakedness for all to see. No longer shall they tinkle with self-assurance as they walk. For the Lord will strip away their artful beauty and their ornaments, their necklaces and bracelets and veils of shimmering gauze. Gone shall be their scarves and ankle chains, headbands, earrings, and perfumes; their rings and jewels, and party clothes and negligees and capes and ornate combs and purses; their mirrors, lovely lingerie, beautiful dresses and veils. Instead of smelling of sweet perfume, they'll stink; for sashes they'll use ropes; their well-set hair will all fall out; they'll wear sacks instead of robes. All their beauty will be gone; all that will be left to them is shame and disgrace. Their husbands shall die in battle; the women, ravaged, shall sit crying on the ground. (TLB)

One day God will reveal the shallowness of the world of fashion and flair. The ugliness of the worldly woman will then show through. Her weak points will be magnified. She will cry, embarrassed and ashamed. Everyone will know the truth that she tried to hide with mascara and pancake makeup.

Her treatment in "God's Ugly Shop" will only be a fitting judgment. Will you go ahead and trust in your "beauty"? If so, God has made an appointment for you.

Beauty Is Vain, But...

A woman that feareth the Lord, she shall be praised. (Proverbs 31:30)

Dr. Paul Adolph said:

Many a life is controlled, or is out of control, as the case may be, by reason of fear. We are fearful that friends will fail us. We are fearful that sickness will come, bringing hardship. We are fearful that we cannot hold out. We are fearful that our national mistakes will catch up with us. We are fearful that our personal mistakes will be our ruin. On every side we are surrounded by fears.[2]

Fear may produce severe emotional tension and disease. Anxiety and worry are forms of fear which sometimes focus on imaginary situations that usually never even come to pass.

The Bible commands us to "Fear not" (Luke 12:7). First Peter 3:6 admonishes us, "Do not give way to fear" (NIV). Why, then, does Proverbs 31:30 say, "A woman that feareth the Lord, she shall be praised"? Don't we have enough fears without acquiring another one?

God's secret of security is in one fear. This one fear can overcome all other fears. "The secret of the Lord is with them that fear Him; and He will show them His covenant" (Psalm 25:14). This command to fear God permeates the Scriptures from beginning to end.

Exodus 18:21	Moreover thou shalt provide out of all the people able men, such as fear God.
2 Chronicles 19:7	Let the fear of the Lord be upon you.
Psalm 147:11	The Lord taketh pleasure in them that fear him.
Ecclesiastes 12:13	Fear God, and keep His commandments; for this is the whole duty of man.
Isaiah 8:12b-14a	Neither fear ye their fear, nor be afraid.

Sanctify the LORD of hosts Himself; and let Him be your fear, and let Him be your dread. And He shall be for a sanctuary.

Matthew 10:28   But rather fear Him who is able to destroy both soul and body in hell.

Acts 10:35   In every nation he that feareth Him, and worketh righteousness, is accepted with Him.

Hebrews 12:28   Let us have grace, whereby we may serve God acceptably with reverence and godly fear.

Revelation 14:7   Fear God, and give glory to Him.

What does it mean to fear God? "It involves a reverential trust in God, accompanied by a hatred of evil."[3] Proverbs 8:13 clearly states, "The fear of the LORD is to hate evil." Charles Haddon Spurgeon said, "Pay to Him humble, childlike reverence, walk in His laws, have respect to His will, tremble to offend Him, hasten to serve Him....Fear God and nothing else."

One of God's object lessons to teach us how to fear Him is the father-child relationship. I had a deep, loving trust in my daddy. I did not want to disappoint him. I desired his approval. Because of the kind of daddy he was, he deserved my respect. I knew he was the head of our family. He was the one who provided food, shelter, and clothing for us. He was faithful and loving in all he did. I trusted him implicitly.

There was another side to my respect however. To this day I would not think of being disrespectful to my father. I feared the consequences of saying or doing the wrong thing. It was enough for me to observe his displeasure with my brothers. I did not want to find out for myself.

Most people do not fear God because they do not know what He is like. They visualize Him as an old grandfather, tottering around heaven. We need to realize that He is the thrice holy God of Israel. He is omnipotent, omniscient,

and omnipresent. He will not overlook sin. We should fear
His displeasure. Hebrews 10:31 says, "It is a fearful thing
to fall into the hands of the living God." To the unbelieving
there is a "certain fearful looking for of judgment and fiery
indignation" (Hebrews 10:27).

God's children, who disobey Him, also have something
to fear. Although they will experience the mercy of God in
relation to eternal punishment, they can look forward to
the sure chastening of the Lord during this life. But God's
chastening is given because He loves us. He wants us to
share in His holiness. He is making us into His image
through His corrective measures (Hebrews 12:5-15).

I believe that the best word to describe God is not love
or mercy, even though He is these, but holiness! Evil is the
antithesis of holiness. If we are to be like Him, then we
must learn to hate evil. "Let us cleanse ourselves from all
filthiness of the flesh and spirit, perfecting holiness in the
fear of God" (2 Corinthians 7:1).

How can we, who are deceitful and desperately
wicked, discover the evil that lurks in our hearts? We must
turn to the God of holiness and let Him reveal these
hidden recesses. Oswald Chambers said,

> The characteristic of the holiness of Almighty God is that it is
> absolute; it is impossible. To antagonize or strain it. The
> characteristic of the holiness of Jesus is that it manifested itself
> by means of antagonism; it was a holiness that could be tested.

> The Son of God, as Son of Man, transformed innocence into
> holy character bit by bit as things opposed; He did not exhibit
> an immutable holiness but a holiness of which we can be
> partakers – "that we might be partakers of His Holiness"
> (Hebrews 12:10). Jesus Christ revealed what a normal man
> should be and in so doing showed how we may become all that
> God wants us to be.[4]

In contrast, God is loving, compassionate, and ready
to forgive and provide for those who fear Him. The follow-

ing are some of the *promised provisions* to those who fear
God:

- ❖ Strong confidence and a place of refuge (Proverbs 14:26)
- ❖ A fountain of life (Proverbs 14:27)
- ❖ Satisfaction (Proverbs 19:23)
- ❖ Riches and honor and life (Proverbs 22:4)
- ❖ A book of remembrance (Malachi 3:16)
- ❖ A banner (Psalm 60:4)
- ❖ His goodness (Psalm 31:19)
- ❖ Will show His covenant (Psalm 25:14)
- ❖ Prolonged days (Proverbs 10:27)
- ❖ Great mercy (Psalm 103:11)

Before we can pursue the path of the wise woman, we
must find a starting place. The Bible says, "The fear of the
LORD is the beginning of knowledge" (Proverbs 1:7).

The fear of God will be expressed both in our attitudes
and in our actions. We will give honor to God through
what we think, what we say, and what we do. The conclu-
sion to what life is all about is expressed in Ecclesiastes
12:13, "Fear God, and keep His commandments; for this is
the whole duty of man."

NOTES

1. T.O. Chisholm, "Oh to Be Like Thee" (Lillenas Publishing Co.,
    © 1957).
2. Paul E. Adolph, *Release from Tension* (Moody Bible Institute of
    Chicago), p. 73.
3. *The New Scofield Reference Bible* (New York: Oxford University
    Press, p. 609), Psalm 19:9 footnote #2.
4. Oswald Chambers, *Still Higher for His Highest* (Fort Washing-
    ton, Pennsylvania: Christian Literature Crusade, 1934, 1970),
    p. 66.

THE MAKING OF
A WISE WOMAN

——•——

UNDER THE SEARCHLIGHT

The path of self-analysis is barren! How often we have made our New Year's resolutions only to have them broken before the day is even over. How empty is our effort! How guilty it makes us. It seems that we felt better before we even began our self-improvement programs. We feel like onions that have been peeled a layer at a time. Underneath each layer there is still more onion.

What utter despair to see our failures and weaknesses, and then be left without a solution. We often cry when we peel onions. Watchman Nee said,

> If all day long we analyze ourselves, dissecting our thoughts and feelings, it will hinder us from losing ourselves In Christ. Unless a believer is deeply taught by the Lord, he will not be able to know himself. Introspection and self-consciousness are harmful to spiritual life.[1]

On the other side of the coin is the self-righteous person who only becomes vain with self-analysis. I became a Christian when I was only nine years old and had not tried many of the sins others indulged in. When the

annual resolution time rolled around, my list of improve-
ments was relatively short.

As the years hurried by how God must have pitied me.
I was only fooling myself. I had areas of my inner self-life
that neither I, nor others, had ever really seen, but He was
ever so patient with me. It was only through an hour of
deep sorrow that I discovered the shallowness of my own
life.

I began a diligent search to know God better. Through
this search God led me to Psalm 139:23-24. I called out,
"Search me, O God, and know my heart; try me, and know
my thoughts: See if there be any wicked way in me, and
lead me in the way everlasting."

God alone can turn on the light within. I see only the
outward issues, but God can see my attitudes and motives.
God has 20:20 vision in the dark. He turns on the search-
light so we can see. He will not "flip the switch" unless we
ask Him. Why waste His energy if we are going to remain
blindfolded by pride and indifference?

IN FRONT OF GOD'S MIRROR

Examine me, O Lord, and prove me; try my reins and my
heart. (Psalm 26:2)

Pick up the mirror of God's Word and take a look at
yourself. Ask God's Holy Spirit to help you see the "real
you." Each of us must deal with the sin question in a
heart-searching manner before we are able to trust God
with the rest of our lives. God must teach us to hate evil so
that we might be free to love good.

You may use the exam on the next few pages as a
guide:

Exam
(Check one or more as indicated)

I am
- ❏ a growing Christian.
- ❏ a backslidden Christian.
- ❏ not a Christian.

I spend more time
- ❏ studying my Bible.
- ❏ reading the newspaper.
- ❏ reading secular magazines.
- ❏ other _____

I pray
- ❏ every day.
- ❏ sometimes.
- ❏ just in emergencies.
- ❏ other _____

I attend church
- ❏ two or more times a week.
- ❏ once a week.
- ❏ at least once a month.
- ❏ about twice a year.
- ❏ other _____

I give to the Lord
- ❏ a tenth and more of my income.
- ❏ a tenth of my income.
- ❏ whatever I feel I can afford.
- ❏ very little.
- ❏ other _____

I witness for the Lord
- ❏ whenever I find or can make opportunity.
- ❏ during revival meetings.
- ❏ hardly ever.
- ❏ never.
- ❏ other _____

I serve the Lord through the church
- ❑ in one or more capacities every week.
- ❑ whenever asked to do something special.
- ❑ never.
- ❑ other _____

I have
- ❑ no unconfessed sin in my life.
- ❑ at least one sin I refuse to confess.
- ❑ many sins in my life.

The following sins trouble me often:
- ❑ self pity
- ❑ manipulation
- ❑ self-consciousness
- ❑ pride
- ❑ retaliation
- ❑ hatred
- ❑ gluttony
- ❑ resentment
- ❑ lying
- ❑ doubt
- ❑ other_____
- ❑ gossip
- ❑ argumentativeness
- ❑ rebellion
- ❑ selfishness
- ❑ impatience
- ❑ slothfulness
- ❑ jealousy
- ❑ lust
- ❑ critical spirit
- ❑ exaggeration

I give priority to
- ❑ my husband and children over other pursuits of my own.
- ❑ to my separate vocation.

My time spent teaching my children spiritual things is
- ❑ adequate.
- ❑ not enough.
- ❑ not at all.

My husband and I pray together
- ❑ often.
- ❑ sometimes.
- ❑ seldom.
- ❑ never.

My husband and I discuss the Bible and spiritual things
- ❑ often.
- ❑ sometimes.
- ❑ seldom.
- ❑ never.

Our family has devotions together
- ❑ often.
- ❑ sometimes.
- ❑ seldom.
- ❑ never.

EVIDENCES OF A CHANGED LIFE

Let me share with you how the Holy Spirit's fullness changed my life.

1. Jesus Christ became more real and precious than He had ever been before. I now had a desire to know Him – as He really is. My life became wonderful and exciting. I was always discovering new and glorious truths about Him. Fellowship with Him became sweet.

2. I did not become sinless, but a hunger for true holiness (moral likeness of Jesus) was implanted within me. This involved so much more than my list of do's and don'ts. The Lord drew to my attention area after area in my self-life that I had barely noticed before. He showed me that I had been subconsciously proud of my own goodness and that it had made me intolerant of those who continued to live in the things that I did not do. He revealed to me my fear, lack of patience, and my self-pity. He showed me that I did not have His kind of love.

3. The Devil became very real to me as I began to trust Christ for victory. He was not going to give up the fight easily. He tried to make my eyes dim and my ears dull to the fact that there is a life of victory. I discovered

that when I trust Jesus, He does "battle" for me. His blood was sufficient for both my past sins and my present sins. I came to realize that Jesus can daily deliver me from sin because, "He ever liveth to make intercession for them [me]" (Hebrews 7:25b).

4. I realized that I had not been allowing Christ to control my life. I had been making my plans and asking God to bless them. He showed me that if I would just let *Him* be in control, I could live victoriously. One of the greatest truths I ever learned was that without Christ I am nothing. It was a hard lesson – for all my life my teachers and my friends had told me, "Joyce, you'll be something one day." He had to show me that the only way I could be anything was if He was everything. Norman Grubb put it this way, "Not to become something, but to contain Someone."

5. I began to talk to others about Jesus Christ. I had been able to go in my own strength and invite people to church and Sunday School, but talking to them about their personal experience with Jesus Christ scared me to death. I am still not all I should be in this area, but I praise Him that He showed me that I can't win people to Christ. Only the Holy Spirit can do that. I've learned to pray something like this, "Lord, You know what a coward I am, and I don't know what to say, but if You will just be with me and give me the words I'll tell this person about Your love. I'm available Lord. I'm trusting You to help me for I know that You will not let me down."

I've come away rejoicing from experiences when I knew God spoke *through* me, times when I never would have had enough courage to say anything at all.

Perhaps your life has been like mine. If it has, I pray that these words might encourage you to "stop trying" to please God and "start trusting" Him for a life of victory.

Since I Thy love have known
Nought else can satisfy;
The fullness of Thy love alone
For this, for this, I cry.[2]

WORKING OUT WHAT GOD HAS WORKED IN

Some women are very content to remain on the first basic level of Christian living. They are experience-oriented, thinking only about what God can do for them. They feel safe and secure just knowing that they are not going to hell.

From this basic level of Christian living it is very easy to dart back and forth into worldly living. Since these women are "better" than the women in the world they never see the need in their own lives. God may have to allow difficulties to come their way to show them their need for Him. If you are in this position, let me urge you to begin the adventure of "knowing Him."

This pursuit involves many levels of Christian living. The Holy Spirit becomes your personal guidance counselor. He is present at each new level, beckoning you on to new heights.

Discovery of truth is the means God uses to help you out of your difficulties and onto a new level of Christian living. God first enlightens your spirit with a new truth. Then your mind reasons it out. The truth seems to grip your life as never before. You see an inner vision, not your own.

You will be so excited and eager to share your new insights, but there must be a time in your life for the reality of working out what God has worked in.

PRACTICE MAKES PERFECT

God gives new revelations to your spirit. This does not necessarily mean that you can immediately practice these new revelations in your daily life. Indeed there may be times of faltering and failing. Discovering spiritual truth and practicing spiritual truth are two different things. Therefore when failures follow, you may tend to doubt the reality of these truths.

You might turn aside, thinking God has failed. It is not God's failure, but your own misconception of what the Christian life is all about. Salvation is a reality, but there is still a lifetime of growth ahead of you. Paul expressed it in this manner, "Work out your own salvation with fear and trembling" (Philippians 2:12). Proverbs 31:31 says that a woman's "own works praise her in the gates." A wise woman is diligently working out God's will in her life day-by-day, step-by-step.

Only a Step

Only a step
Just one step
at a time
Don't let me
walk ahead of You
Nor linger far behind
I look out far ahead
and cannot see;
Oh Jesus Christ,
One step with You
is quite enough
for me.

GOURMET LIVING

God did not say, "work *for* your salvation." God said, "work *out* your salvation" (Philippians 2:12, italics mine). You must possess it before you can work it out.

Suppose that you are given a brand-new food processor and bags of groceries. These hold a profusion of potential breads, puddings, and souffles, but you must work out these delicious delights in your kitchen before they can truly be yours.

God gives to you the gift of eternal life through His Son, Jesus Christ. You must work this gift out in your own life.

Practice in cooking brings about improvement in performance. This is also true in the Christian life. You must learn basic skills first. You must experiment with simple recipes before you proceed to entertain fifty guests for a gourmet dinner.

You will find that there will be definite crisis experiences in your Christian life where you will commit yourself to new dimensions of Christian living. These will differ in their impact on your life in accordance with your background and temperament.

It is at these intervals that God will meet you and beckon you to "more." You can either say "yes" or "no" to God when He beckons you to "come up higher." If you do say "yes" you will find that new level of Christian living to be unfamiliar ground. You won't be comfortable there. You will stumble and fall more often. But with practice, God will work your life into continual gracious gourmet living. You will see that practice makes perfect.

Oswald Chambers said this about the concept of sanctification:

> The great need today among those of us who profess sanctification is the patience and ability to work out the holiness of God in every detail of the life. When we are first adjusted to God it is on the great big general lines; then the Holy Spirit educates us down to the scruples. He makes us sensitive to things we never thought of before. No matter what our experience may be, we must beware of the curse of being stationary; we have to go on and on in the holy life until we manifest the disposition God has given us in every detail of our lives. The disposition of Jesus enables us to keep all the commandments of God, not some of them.[3]

Spiritual Contaminants And Divine Decontaminants[4]

You may have the right ingredients for a gourmet feast, but if your hands are dirty the food will be contaminated with germs. This could bring about illness and death instead of life.

At this point in your spiritual life you are probably appalled at the grosser sins like adultery, stealing, and drunkenness. All of these sins, however, have their beginning in more "respectable sins." You might even call them "bad attitudes." I will refer to them as "spiritual contaminants."

Examine with me four of these contaminants that are likely to defile the Christian woman as she goes about to "work out her salvation." Let's look at the remedies from God's point of view.

Contaminant –
The Pollution Of Perfectionism

Paul cautioned against the attitude of trying to be perfect in the energy of the flesh. In Galatians 3:3 he said, "Are ye so foolish? Having begun in the Spirit, are ye now made perfect by the flesh?"

Dr. Paul E. Adolph defines perfectionism this way: "An attitude that represents dissatisfaction with any achievement or person that is short of perfection, regardless of how fitted or ill-fitted he is to attain to it."[5]

Here is a checklist to help you discover if you are a perfectionist:

❖ Are you extremely critical?

❖ Are you the type of person who cannot sit down at night until every piece of misplaced clutter is put into its exact place?

❖ Do you apologize when someone comes to your house and the house is not really messed up, you just have not dusted that day?

❖ Do you begin jobs that you are not capable of, and then get frustrated?

❖ When you cannot complete a task satisfactorily, are you always trying to find an excuse or blaming someone else for your failure?

❖ Do you expect spiritual perfection in others and yourself?

Keep in mind that there are many levels of perfectionism. However, it is hard to see perfectionism in one's self.

This type person will suffer from now until eternity. Immediately there is the possibility of an emotional tension pattern, usually of the stiff-neck type.[4] This person has an unbending attitude. In its extreme, it can result in a nervous breakdown. This woman usually does not recognize the source of her tension. Perfectionism seems like such a good quality to her.

In eternity her perfectionistic attitude will result in no true fruit or reward. Those works done for the glory of her own self will only become "wood, hay, and stubble" (1 Corinthians 3:12). They will all be burned up.

DIVINE DECONTAMINANT – THE STRENGTH OF THE SPIRIT

It is God that girdeth me with strength, and maketh my way perfect. (Psalm 18:32)

The Holy Spirit is needed to counteract perfectionism. You should stop trying and start trusting. Stop playing God in your own life and in the lives of others.

I always wanted to be the "perfect" minister's wife. Anytime I heard someone say what a minister's wife ought to be or do I made a mental note of it. After some years I had accumulated an impossible invisible list of do's and don'ts.

I had always loved my role. Therefore, it was very difficult for me to admit to myself years later that I was no

longer happy with the position. I finally discovered that
each woman is a different individual. There is no ready-
made list for a perfect minister's wife. Some are suited for
entertaining large groups of people; others are suited to a
quiet counseling ministry. Some are dynamic leaders in
the ladies' work; others are gifted in the preschool area.
Some are outgoing; some are quiet. Some are multi-
talented; others are one-talent Christians.

I discovered that the "perfect" minister's wife (as well
as the "perfect" anybody's wife) should discover who she is
and what *her* talents and spiritual gifts are. She should
then be the best of whatever particular "model" God has
picked out for her. Trying to measure up to the impossible
dream will only bring frustration.

Don't forget that God majors in things that *seem*
impossible. I have seen the Lord take many impossible
areas in my own life and transform them. When I have
dared to trust Him, He has enabled me to do things that I
know are beyond my natural capacities. He has enlarged
my life that I might be adequate. The only prerequisite is
that I do these things in the power and the strength of the
Holy Spirit. If I do, then God will continue making me into
what He wants me to become. "Man is a vessel destined to
receive God; a vessel which must be enlarged as it is filled
and filled in proportion as it is enlarged." – Godet

How can you know the difference between serving in
your strength and serving in God's strength? There is a
key, for no frustration or tension results when serving in
the strength of the Spirit! "I will go in the strength of the
Lord GOD" (Psalm 71:16).

SPIRITUAL CONTAMINANT –
THE BONDAGE OF BITTERNESS

If you harbor a grudge in your heart, be it ever so
small, it will begin to take hold of you. You will begin to be

wrapped in the bondage of bitterness. The longer you keep your grudge, the more difficult it will become to set yourself free from the root system that has entangled itself around you, choking the spiritual life out of you.

Hebrews 12:15 contains this caution, "Looking diligently....lest any root of bitterness springing up trouble you, and thereby many be defiled." Bitterness is pictured here as having roots. Be assured that it will only bring forth weeds.

The Root Of Bitterness

Don't let bitterness take root
    in the depths of your heart
But instead let His Spirit
    loving forgiveness impart.
If you treasure just one little
    grudge overnight
It can grow and sprout roots
    which are all out of sight.
Others may not see these roots
    taking hold
Like tentacles grasping
    your soul to enfold.

As you cherish and water your
    fast growing seed
One day soon it will sprout
    to be but a weed!

Don't try by yourself to
    jerk up this weed
You may snap the top
    and thus growth impede –

But still underground the roots
    will be growing
The others can't see, they
    soon will be knowing.

> Let *God* pull this weed with
> all of *His* might.
> Let His love smooth the ground
> then all will be right!

Leave vengeance to God. Don't steal what belongs to him. " 'Vengeance is mine: I will repay,' saith the Lord" (Romans 12:19).

Most bitterness comes from simple misunderstanding of supposed wrongs. Some bitterness is the result of genuine wrongdoing on the part of someone else. Even if you have been genuinely wronged, only emotional harm can come to you through resentment instead of forgiveness.

DIVINE DECONTAMINANT –
THE LOVE OF THE SPIRIT

The love of the Spirit is what is clearly needed to overcome these insidious attitudes. But first you must be willing. You must choose to forgive. Then you must confess your own helplessness. Invite Jesus to take over and forgive through you. It is truly a miraculous procedure.

A bitter spirit will infect everyone around you. The beautiful Rose of Sharon will slowly but surely become choked out. In His place will grow wickedness and weeds. You will lose both your capacity to forgive others and your capacity to receive forgiveness from God (Matthew 6:12).

SPIRITUAL CONTAMINANT –
THE IRRITANT OF INDECISION

Wherefore be ye not unwise, but understanding what the will of the Lord is. (Ephesians 5:17)

The increased tempo of modern living leaves little time for meditation and evaluation. Sometimes you can become so busy that you accomplish next to nothing.

I had a friend whose stomach was literally in knots. She was suffering from colon trouble, backache, and other problems. The doctor told her that she was doing too much. I asked her if she had ever invited Jesus into her life. She said that she had as a little child, but that she had gotten away from Him. She knew that she needed to get right with Him and get back into church. She worked at a full-time job and was the mother of three active children. She kept the house and did all the extra things that came up. Besides all this she was on a bowling league with her husband! She had no time for God and Christian activities.

You see, a wise woman must get her priorities right! If she doesn't have time for prayer, Bible study, ministry to others, and church, then her life is all mixed up. She is going to have to completely rearrange everything, or she will be a real *setup* for an emotional *letdown*.

My friend prayed with me that Jesus would become the center of her life, and she thanked me for coming. I trusted the Lord to work out the details in her life, but it was her decision. She had to begin!

"Oh," you may say, "I am not like that. I may be caught up in the feverish activity circle, but at least most of it is centered around the church." You may be one of the many women who indiscriminately accept every request that comes to you inside the church. You work until your body is weary and emotional tension is built up. Because of your harmful emotional condition you become confused. You think that you have been serving God, but now your strength is sapped and your motivation is gone. You do not know what you should do and so you dwell in indecision.

DIVINE DECONTAMINANT – THE LEADING OF THE SPIRIT

A wise woman should not try to acquire a list of accomplishments; she should simply center her activities around the will of God. To discover His will she must experience the leading of the Spirit. He speaks in a small inner voice. She must be still before Him to hear.

Jesus did not heal every sick person, raise every dead person, and eat in everyone's home. Jesus did only what the Father sent Him to do (see John 6:38). When you do only those things He is leading you to do, the result is a restful peace of mind. There are two little letters right in the middle of the alphabet which provide a woman a solution to her problems. They are N-O! If she cannot learn to say "no" by herself she should ask her husband to help her evaluate her activities. She should then follow his advice as her spiritual leader.

I used to think that every nomination committee was led of God. I have discovered that is not so. Many leaders do not wait on the leading of the Holy Spirit. They become desperate and take the best available people to fill vacant positions. You must discover on your own what is the will of the Lord. The committee may be Spirit-led or it may not be. You must find God's will for you on your own.

You may be doing too much; you may not be doing enough. You must stay close to the Savior in order to guard against either extreme. You must save time to fellowship with Him and save time to study His Word and meditate upon it. If you will listen to Him speak through His Word, you will learn to discern His guiding hand in every circumstance. If you are a "Meatloaf Martha," maybe it's time to change to a "Manna Mary."

SPIRITUAL CONTAMINANT – THE DIRT OF DISCONTENT

Failure to rejoice in the Lord will result in a spirit of discontentment. You will resent the circumstances in which the Lord has placed you. You may either feel incapable of dealing with your own "opportunities" or you may feel envious of the opportunities that others have. You may covet the possessions and attainments of others and complain at your own sorrow, sickness, and setbacks.

If you could only realize that each woman has her own job to do. The Holy Spirit gives to each woman the gifts that He wants her to have. We need each other! "But now hath God set the members every one of them in the body, as it hath pleased Him" (1 Corinthians 12:18).

You shouldn't be discouraged if you are not doing what God has called someone else to do. You should praise God when difficulties come.

A spirit of discontentment breeds a critical eye. You become like the man with Limburger cheese on his moustache. He concluded, "The whole world stinks."

DIVINE DECONTAMINANT – THE SUFFICIENCY OF THE SPIRIT

Not that we are sufficient of ourselves . . . but our sufficiency is of God. (2 Corinthians 3:5)

You experience the "sufficiency of the Spirit" through your "sixth sense" – that of faith. Faith is believing God in the dark. Faith is believing God even when everything and everybody cries out, "He is not here."

You must discover the life-changing principle of "blessing the Lord at all times," or "giving thanks in everything."

It was in a desperate hour of sorrow that God began to reprogram my Christian life. Without time for us even to pray, death reached down into the crib and snatched our "little one" away. I didn't know what to do or what to say. All I could do was "hold on to Jesus."

As I was clinging to Him, He reminded me that there was help and comfort in His Word. In the days to follow I began to live in the Book. As I did, Jesus began to show me what I should do and what I should say. He pointed me to Psalm 34:1, "I will bless the LORD at all times; His praise

shall continually be in my mouth." He showed me 1
Thessalonians 5:18, "In every thing give thanks; for this is
the will of God in Christ Jesus concerning you."

It was the will of God for me to give thanks in *every-thing!* I began to try in my own way, in my own words to
give thanks for this situation. I tried to bless the Lord, but I
felt like such a fake – a hypocrite! I did not feel thankful
and I did not feel like praising God.

It was then that the Lord showed me that He had not
asked me to feel thankful, but just to do it – just to obey
Him. I discovered that if I could not find and believe my
own words, that I was perfectly free to use His words. He
said to me inwardly, "Don't fake it – faith it." I began to do
just that. I gave the Lord's own words back to Him as an
offering of thanksgiving and praise. I did not immediately
feel the reality of what I was doing, but I no longer felt like a
fake. I knew His words were true.

The more I used His words the deeper He led me into
them. He taught me to say with Job, "The LORD gave, and
the LORD hath taken away; blessed be the name of the LORD"
(Job 1:21). He led me to say with the Psalmist, "Because
Thy lovingkindness is better than life, my lips shall praise
Thee. Thus will I bless Thee while I live; I will lift up my
hands in Thy name" (Psalm 63:3-4).

"Better than life, Lord? I thought life was the most
priceless possession I could have."

"Better than life, my child!"

These words would cut across my very soul as I offered
them to God. Nevertheless, day after day I "faithed" my
praise and thanksgiving. He began embedding their reality
deep within my heart. I do not know whether it was in the
weeks or in the months to follow, but one day I actually felt
the reality of what I had been saying.

Today, I can say with my own words and all the reality
of my soul, "Thank you, Lord, for the darkest hour of my
life. Praise Your holy name!"

My life has not been the same since then. I had learned a whole new concept of living – total dependence on Jesus Christ. It was just the beginning of a growth process that has never ended.

He took me up higher than I had ever been before. I learned that I could "faith it" from any plateau, but I had to learn to live on that higher plane. That would take time. It would be a daily process.

Oswald Chambers describes life on the higher plane as something that looks at first like a steep pinnacle we are desperately trying to hold onto. But, he says,

> In our spiritual life God does not provide pinnacles on which we stand like spiritual acrobats; He provides tablelands of easy and delightful security. Recall the conception you had of holiness before you stood by the grace of God where you do today, it was the conception of a breathless standing on a pinnacle for a second at a time, but never with the thought of being able to live there.

> But – when the Holy Spirit brought you there, you found it was not a pinnacle, but a plateau, a broad way, where the provision of strength and peace comes all the time, a much easier place to live than lower down.[6]

The path to true wisdom is found in the many invitations to "come up higher," as in the chorus of the hymn, "Higher Ground" by Johnson Oatman, Jr.

> Lord, lift me up and let me stand,
> By faith, on heaven's tableland,
> A higher plane than I have found;
> Lord, plant my feet on higher ground.

Come Up Higher

"Come up higher," the Savior called,
"And live with Me *above* the clouds.
You can see much better from where *I* am!

"The mountain tops are glorious –
    You not only see the shadows
        in the valleys,
    But the sunlight gleaming
        on the lofty peaks.
"You can never catch the full
    splendor of My glory
        down below –
But from up here you catch a glimpse
    of so much more . . .
            The changing of the colors
                from gray to white to
                    rosy pink
            As the sun dances on the
                clouds and
                    snow.
            You'll look with breathless awe
                at clouds – like drifts of
                    newly fallen snow –
            Then at majestic mountains
                with their snow-capped crowns.
            Suddenly the earth appears with
                not a cloud in sight –
                    so clear that you can even see
                        the trees far
                            down below."
"Oh, how can I live above the clouds,
    And see these glorious scenes?
I could never reach up there –
    You can see I don't have wings."
"Come, my child, I'll lift you
    on My wings –
Just take my hand and upward we
    will soar.
            Up, Up through these thick,
                gray clouds where
                    nothing you can see.
            There's nothing to make you feel afraid,

For I'll hold on to you.
In just a little while you'll see the view
From where *I* see.

"Then all the trials of life
you'll understand;
They're but a part of the
glorious picture
Of a life spent down below.
"They only help to make the
beauty that we can
fully see when
viewed from
up above!"

"Yes, Lord, I want to go up higher
And live with *You*;
Not only when I die
But today –
Here Lord, take my hand;
I'm trusting You to lift me to
Your vantage point . . .
Then I'll see more clearly
And really understand!"

No, I don't understand why God uses the "dark" hours, the troublesome times, the irksome people, and the irritating circumstances to make me into His image. I am willing to leave that in His hands until later. Then I will ask Him. Yes, "I'll ask the reasons; He'll tell me why/when we talk it over in the bye and bye."[7]

I know that it works. When I have chosen by faith to practice God's principle of blessing the Lord at all times and giving thanks in everything, it has always worked. He is sufficient for every need. From Him I have received peace, power, and growth in my Christian life. It has been the times when I have not chosen to practice this prin-ciple that have been the most frustrating times in my life. I only have two choices. I can either try to figure things out on my own or I can try godly wisdom – looking from God's point of view (see Proverbs 3:5-6).

Have you discovered this life-changing principle? If not, begin today. Bless the Lord and give thanks in whatever circumstance you find yourself right now. If this is a joyous time in your life and you feel like praising – great! If not – don't *fake* it; *faith* it. Here, use these words, God's own words. Remember that they are true!

"Bless the LORD, O my soul; and all that is within me, bless His holy name."
Psalm 103:1

"Every day will I bless Thee; and I will praise Thy name for ever and ever."
Psalm 145:2

"O God, my heart is fixed; I will sing and give praise, even with my glory."
Psalm 108:1

"I will praise the name of God with a song, and will magnify him with thanksgiving."
Psalm 69:30

NOTES

1. Watchman Nee, *The Spiritual Man* (New York: Christian Fellowship Publishers, Inc. 1968) I, 10.
2. J. Sidlow Baxter, *Going Deeper* (Grand Rapids, Michigan: Zondervan Publications, 1959), p. 30. Used by permission.
3. Oswald Chambers, *Still Higher for His Highest* (Fort Washington, Pennsylvania: Christian Literature Crusade, 1934, 1970), p. 80.
4. The general concept of "spiritual contaminants" was drawn from *Release from Tension* by Paul Adolph (Chicago: Moody Press, 1956), pp. 63-136.
5. Ibid., p. 65
6. Oswald Chambers, *The Moral Foundations of Life* (Fort Washington, Pennsylvania: Oswald Chambers Publications Association and Christian Literature Crusade, 1934) p. 32
7. Ira Stamphill, "We'll Talk It Over," Golden Series Collection (Winona Lake: Rodeheaver, © 1949).

CHAPTER THREE

A WOMAN'S
SOURCE OF WISDOM

THE LIVING WORD OF GOD

Jesus Only

Once it was the blessing,
  Now it is the Lord;
Once it was the feeling,
  Now it is His Word;
Once His gifts I wanted,
  Now Himself alone;
Once I sought for healing,
  Now the healer own.

Once 'twas painful trying,
  Now 'tis perfect trust;
Once a half salvation,
  Now the uttermost;
Once 'twas ceaseless holding,
  Now He holds me fast;
Once 'twas constant drifting,
  Now my anchor's cast.

Once 'twas busy planning,
  Now 'tis trustful prayer.

Once 'twas anxious caring,
Now He has the care;
Once 'twas what I wanted,
Now what Jesus says;
Once 'twas constant asking,
Now 'tis ceaseless praise.

Once it was my working,
His it hence shall be;
Once I tried to use Him,
Now He uses me;
Once the power I wanted,
Now the mighty One;
Once I worked for glory,
Now His will alone.[1]

AN INNER GLIMPSE OF HIM

I placed my focus on Jesus and as a result His reality
gripped my life. For the first time I saw myself as I really
was, and I didn't look so good. I saw my self-righteousness
so clearly. It was all filthy rags in His sight (see Isaiah 64:6).
I had been living my Christian life in my own strength and
consequently getting the glory that should have gone to
Jesus.

I had thought I was too good to be bad. But when I saw
Him in His glory, I knew what the apostle Paul meant when
he said that he was the chief of sinners (see 1 Timothy
1:15). I thought that had been just a pious declaration. Now
I felt exactly the same way.

I asked the Lord for His cleansing and then for His
filling. I believe that He heard and answered the prayer of
my searching, longing heart. The book, We Would See Jesus,
by Roy and Revel Hession, was greatly used in my life. It
showed me the importance of simply "looking to Jesus."
Imprinted on its cover and indelibly on my heart are these
words: "It is enough to see Jesus and to go on seeing Him."[2]

It was by "seeing" Jesus that I had received the very life of God in the first place. To "go on seeing Him" was how I would continue to grow in this relationship.

YOUR MATE – THE INTEGRAL FORCE OF MARRIAGE

The marriage relationship is an illustration of this spiritual truth. When you enter the door of matrimony your mate is in the center of your focus, but gradually your aim changes. You make a startling discovery. It is not all moonlight and roses. There are meals to be cooked, floors to be swept, dishes to be washed, and laundry to be done.

Then a little baby enters your life. The baby has to be fed, diapers have to be washed and folded. Then another baby and perhaps another arrive. The workload is increased. You suddenly discover that you have little time for your "beloved." He likewise has had his time for you stolen by responsibilities outside the home. One day you realize that you need to readjust your goals for your marriage. You sit down with pen in hand:

"Let's see,

1. I must be a better housekeeper – since the "kids" came, things have become a wreck.

2. I must be a better cook – I have been fixing too many potpies and frozen dinners. Where does the time go?

3. I must be a better mother – with so many "little ones" my patience has run so thin.

4. I must take some time for myself – I need to lose ten extra pounds and I need a new hairstyle. Perhaps even a hobby would help.

5. And, oh yes, I must find some time to be together with my husband."

Now I know that you didn't actually make that list and leave your husband in last place, but have you done it unconsciously? Has he become just one of the many things in your life? Could he even have become last?

If this is true in your union it is no wonder that marriage has become a drag. No wonder you are bored to death with monotonous routine. You didn't arrive at the marriage altar because you loved to wash dishes and sweep floors. I hope you arrived there for the same reason I did – because you loved your husband so much that you couldn't stand to be apart. All these incidentals held some joy when he was at the center of your relationship.

❖ Do you remember – how you thought of *him* even before you got dressed? You asked yourself what colors *he* liked and what *his* favorite dress was?

❖ Do you remember – how you anticipated the times when you would be alone to talk and share your love with *him*?

❖ Do you remember – when *he* was what "it" was all about?

He wasn't just *one* of the parts of your marriage. He was the integral force in every facet. Such a oneness is true marriage. Consciously and unconsciously he is in your mind and heart at all times. You can never forget him. After years of marriage you can almost know what he is thinking.

OUR SPIRITUAL HUSBAND

It is the same with the church's spiritual husband – Jesus Christ. He can't be just one factor on your list or possibly even the last factor. That isn't a fulfilling Christian life. The goals for your Christian life can't be:

1. Living a good life;
2. Serving others;
3. Experiencing joy and peace;
4. Going to heaven.

Inside the cover of the life-changing book, *We Would See Jesus*, I was met with the following statement, which helped to revolutionize my life:

My Goal

My goal is God Himself
Not joy, nor peace
Nor even blessing
But Himself, my God![2]

I adopted these words for my goal. I copied them in the flyleaf of my Bible. But more than that I etched them on my heart. That has been many years ago and the goal of my life has never changed. My lifelong adventure of getting to know and love Jesus has been entirely satisfying. "It is enough to see Jesus and go on seeing Him."[2]

HOW DO YOU SEE JESUS?

If "it is enough to see Jesus and to go on seeing Him," we must consider the question: How do you see Him?

1. *Look for Jesus on every page of His wonderful written Word.* This will be considered further in the next chapter, for it is so vitally important.

2. *Ask the Spirit of God to reveal Jesus as you read His Word.* It is His job to do this (John 16:13-14). You can memorize the words and intellectually tell others what Jesus is like, but until your spirit is vitalized by God's Spirit you can never truly be enlightened. Facts without enlightenment can produce a deadening spiritual effect. The Holy Spirit is needed to say "Amen" to these facts and make them real within your inner being.

3. *Commit your life to doing God's will.* Why should God bother to reveal His Son to you if you don't intend to do His will? It would be a waste of His time. Your will should choose to do His will. "When our will runs parallel with the will of God, no cross is formed; but when our will runs counter to God's will, a cross is formed which is heavy to be borne."[3]

4. *Remember that you cannot obey God with your own human effort.* But He can give you the power if you will but trust Him to do so. Major Ian Thomas says that you should say to God: "I can't; You never said I could; You can: You always said You would."[4]

5. *Look for Jesus every day and all day in every circumstance of life.* Develop the habit of looking for Him at all times. *Practicing the Presence of God* relates how Brother Lawrence made it a habit to communicate with God in every duty, however menial.

Andrew Murray said "The love of Jesus must be in the inner chamber, in all my work, in my daily life."[5] In his book *Abide in Christ* he exhorts, "Believer, would you abide in Christ, let it be day by day. A day, just one day only, but still a day, given to abide and grow up in Jesus Christ. In it I may, I must become more closely united to Jesus."[6]

THE WRITTEN WORD OF GOD

SEEING THE BEAUTY OF JESUS IN HIS WORD

These Things

Two forlorn disciples walked
    the Emmaus Road that day –
The day that Christ
    rose from the dead.
As they talked and reasoned
    about "these things,"
Jesus Himself drew near, but
    they didn't recognize
        who He was.

"What 'things' are you
    talking about?" Jesus asked.
They said, "Haven't you heard

how they condemned and
crucified Jesus of Nazareth?
     We believed He was to be
     our redeemer,
          But today is the third day
          since 'these things' were done.
               Some say He is alive,
               But we do not know 'these things'
               for sure."
Then Jesus said,
     "Oh, if you had known the Scriptures,
     you would know 'these things.'
     You would have known that Christ
     would suffer and rise again."
Then He explained in Moses and all
     the prophets "these things"
          about Himself.

"Stay with us tonight," they
     pleaded, "and tell us more."
And so He tarried and blessed
     and broke the bread at
     suppertime that night.
As He broke the bread their
     eyes were opened –
It was Jesus Himself!
But then He vanished out of
     their sight.
They said one to another,
     "Did not out hearts burn
     within us while He
     talked with us –
     as He opened the
     Scriptures along the way?
'These things' were all
     concerning Him!
He is in all the Scriptures –
     In every book
     On every page."

A SKELETON OF FACTS

My college major was religion. I learned a lot of facts about the Bible, but the emphasis was mainly historical. It was almost ten years later that the Lord led me to a new approach to studying the Scriptures. It seems as though I just had a skeleton of facts, and the effect from that is sometimes deadening.

I seldom studied the Old Testament, for it seemed as though there were just too many facts. I thought I had covered the Gospels rather comprehensively because I had taken a course on "The Life of Christ" in college. So it was only rather dutifully that I would read from the Old Testament or the Gospels. I did love the Epistles of Paul because they seemed to be more relevant to my life. For many years I majored on a study of them.

A DEAD BODY COME ALIVE

A combination of factors led to my putting flesh onto these dead bones and life into this dead body of information that I had stored for years in my mind. The major factor, however, was a deep need in my life that caused me to want to go deeper into the Scriptures. Various books and sermons containing a new approach to Bible study also helped me along the way.

This new approach totally transformed my study of the Bible. It was so simple I can't imagine how I missed it the first time. All it involved was "looking for Jesus" in every book of the Bible that I studied – whether in the Old or the New Testament.

A TREASURE HUNT

It became so very exciting! Some of the precious treasure was lying right on the surface, while other treasures were hidden in rocky crevices. Some were in the center of a giant mountain which had to be possessed before the treasures could be uncovered. I determined that all of the wealth would be mine!

This precious treasure was Jesus himself. He is the treasure throughout God's wonderful Book. You must constantly search there to find out who He really is and what He is really like.

Old Testament Discoveries

I began to search for Him in the most unlikely place – the Old Testament. It was in that place that I discovered the most priceless art treasures of Jesus. I could see Him from every angle. I began to recognize the numerous places where He appeared. I saw Him as my Passover Lamb and as my Tabernacle. I saw Him pictured in the lives of Joseph and Isaac. He was everywhere, in every story.

Yes, I have my favorite portraits, and there are some that bless me more than others, but I will never discard even one of them. What I can't see through my limited vision might be the very one drawn for you. The pictures that seem lifeless and stern one day might become animated and joyful at the time I need them the most.

The Gospels – Four Views Of The Savior

It was a combination of a trip to the Holy Land and my own curiosity that sent me back to take a more serious look at the four Gospels. Why were there four of them? What was the purpose behind this?

How thrilled I was to find out that each Gospel contained a different pose of Jesus. I saw Him in: Matthew as the King of the Jews; Mark as the Suffering Servant; Luke as the Son of Man; and John as the Son of God. I studied for nine months in these wonderful books. How could I have ever become bored with these divinely inspired Gospels?

THE SILENT LAMB

Of all the beautiful and awesome portraits that I have viewed down through the years, my very favorite is that of Jesus, my Passover Lamb. Drawn with matchless skill, this portrait is like a tapestry with threads from the Old and New Testaments masterfully interwoven.

This Lamb, the Lamb of God, opened not His mouth. He was silent before His shearers. How could He have allowed sinful, vile men to rail at Him and spit on Him and yet answer not a word? How can I ever explain what this picture has meant in my life and how very much I love Him for remaining silent?

Never A Word

Jesus stood before Pilate,
   His accusers stood near by;
They agreed together to tell
   many things that were not so.
But He answered nothing!

Pilate asked, "Why don't you answer;
   Don't You hear all the things
     they're saying?"
Pilate marveled still that
Jesus answered nothing!

The soldiers then took Jesus
   to the judgment hall –
     They stripped Him
      and robed Him;
     They pressed a crown
      of thorns into His brow;
     They mocked Him and

spat on Him –
Hailed Him as
"King of the Jews"
They reviled Him, but –
He reviled not!

He was brought as a lamb
to the slaughter –
Spotless and perfect
Lamb of God.
But as a sheep who protests
not before her shearers,
So this Lamb opened not His mouth!

Pilate marveled greatly that
He answered not a word!
I, too, can only marvel at this
God-like kind of love.

How unlike the Savior *I*
seem to always be –
With many words I protest and
claim my innocence.

"Oh, make me into Thy likeness!"

I will never comprehend the
Savior's love for me;
That never a word came in defense,
He could not explain
They could not understand
Though sinless –
He was guilty!

My sins were upon Him
I deserved the mocking,
the scourging,
the awful pain.
But He bore it all
And answered never a word!

In Praise Of Jesus

Can't you hear the voice of wisdom? (Proverbs 8:1, TLB)

I believe it is Jesus who calls to you from the book of Proverbs. He invites you to follow Him and find riches and satisfaction through Him, the personification of wisdom. Read and see if you don't feel the same way. Substitute the name of Jesus wherever you find the word "wisdom."

Can't you hear the voice of wisdom (Jesus)? She is standing at the city gates and at every fork in the road, and at the door of every house. Listen to what she says: "Listen, men!" she calls. "How foolish and naïve you are! Let me give you understanding. O foolish ones, let me show you common sense! Listen to me! For I have important information for you. Everything I say is right and true, for I hate lies and every kind of deception. My advice is wholesome and good. There is nothing of evil in it. My words are plain and clear to anyone with half a mind – if it is only open! My instruction is far more valuable than silver or gold.

For the value of wisdom (Jesus) is far above rubies; nothing can be compared with it (Him). Wisdom (Jesus) and good judgment live together, for wisdom (Jesus) knows where to discover knowledge and understanding. If anyone respects and fears God, he will hate corruption and deceit of every kind.

Listen to my counsel – oh, don't refuse it – and be wise. Happy is the man who is so anxious to be with me that he watches for me daily at my gates, or waits for me outside my home! For whoever finds me finds life and wins approval from the Lord. But the one who misses me has injured himself irreparably. Those who refuse me, show that they love death.

Proverbs 8:1-13, 33-36 (TLB)

Proverbs 8:11 declares that "wisdom is better than rubies." Likewise Proverbs 31:10 declares that the price of a virtuous woman is far above rubies. This is because this priceless "wise" woman is filled with none other than Jesus Christ. The New Testament reveals that in Him "are hid all the treasures of wisdom and knowledge" (Colossians 2:3). In 1 Corinthians 1:24, the Bible clearly states that Christ is "the wisdom of God."

Socrates stated, "The Delphic oracle said I was the wisest of all the Greeks. It is because that I alone, of all the Greeks, know that I know nothing." Socrates, who was so wise according to the fashion of this world, has thus admitted to being ignorant. And so he was, for true wisdom is to know that I am nothing, but that God is everything.

God made foolish the wisdom of this world. If you are to be wise, you must turn your eyes from the logic of this so-called liberated age and look solely unto Jesus.

A WOMAN OF THE WORD

A wise woman is filled with the living and written Word of God. I want to be a "woman of the Word." To know and love the living Word I must know His written Word. There is not an easy, lazy way. It must be a daily consistent study. A little knowledge can make you guilty of proof-texting and faulty interpretation. Anyone with fair intelligence can learn facts, but only the "anointing" of the Holy Spirit can teach you truth as you meditate and pray over God's word.

The Bible is full of examples of women who desired to be women of the Word. They listened when God spoke, then they obeyed what they heard. God did marvelous works in the lives of these women.

"HAS GOD SAID?"

Satan has always been trying to cast doubt on God's Word. From the very beginning he developed the strategy of mixing partial truth and partial error. He asked the deceptive question, "Has God said?"

God said to Adam, "You may freely eat of every tree in the garden except the tree of the knowledge of good and evil." One day Satan came to Eve and subtly inquired, "Has God said, you shouldn't eat of every tree of the garden?" (Genesis 3:1, author's translation). Then he told a boldfaced lie about God. He told the woman, "If you eat of that tree you will not surely die."

God had provided all that Eve's heart could ever desire. He created her with a prized position – she was to be a helper, suitable for Adam. He supplied her with every needed provision. He placed her in a literal paradise for an earthly home. However, Eve wasn't satisfied.

One day, probably very bored, she was attracted to a colorful personality who was just waiting for the proper timing to beguile her. The essence of the first woman's sin was that she didn't believe God's Word. She listened instead to the voice of the serpent.

Many a modern woman hasn't really changed. Many are still listening to Satan's subtle slanders against God's Word. He is still asking, "Has God said?"

Has God said, "I want you to be a helper?" (see Genesis 2:18). You know you're just as smart as any man. You can be the leader!

Has God said, "Be a keeper at home?" It is too boring just being a housewife. Going into the factory, the police force, the theater is better. That's where the real action is!

Has God said, "Be obedient to your own husbands?" (see Titus 2:5). You don't have to be submissive to anyone but God. You've been liberated!

Has God said, "I do not want you to have a place of teaching and authority over the man?" (see 1 Timothy 2:12). You're a much more gifted communicator than he. You could make the issues much clearer!

Has God said, "The fruit of the womb is his reward?" (Psalm 127:3). Why, you could ruin your figure. Anyway, children bring such heartache!

God has said many things. Sometimes we aren't listening to hear what He has to say. Other times we hear the message loud and clear, but we rationalize and say that it doesn't apply to us today. He couldn't possibly mean that. Those concepts are so out of date!

God said a crazy thing to a young, unmarried girl named Mary. He actually told her that she was going to have a baby. Besides that, He said she was still going to be a virgin when she was pregnant. That is the most ridiculous, wild claim I have ever heard in my life. Everybody knows that is impossible! Yet this young virgin who did indeed hear the word of God, unbelievable as it was, by faith simply replied, "Behold the handmaid of the Lord; be it unto me according to Thy word" (Luke 1:38).

God's spoken word was then taken by His Spirit and was formed in the very womb of a young woman who simply believed God. I'm sure she must have had her fears, her frustrations, and many lonely days of misunderstanding by her friends and family. I'm sure that they didn't believe that she had received "a word from God." She had not even studied at the synagogue. Surely they thought life for her was going to be very unfulfilling.

Yet for Mary, the one who listened to God's Word, the one who received God's Word, to her was given the highest privilege ever bestowed upon a woman. At God's appointed time she brought forth the living Word of God.

"But Mary kept all these things, and pondered them in her heart" (Luke 2:19).

> Oh to know the heart of Mary,
> What a treasure
> would be found.

But if I receive His Word,
to me
All heavenly blessings
will in me abound!

NOTES

1. A. B. Simpson, Tract #12 (Warminster, Pennsylvania).
2. Roy and Revel Hession, *We Would See Jesus* (Fort Washington, Pennsylvania, 1934).
3. Aughey, quoted in *The World's Best Religious Quotations*, comp. James Gilchrist Lawson (New York: Fleming Revel Co., 1930), p. 188.
4. Quoted from a sermon.
5. Andrew Murray, *God's Best Secrets* (Illinois: Good News Publishers, 1962).
6. Andrew Murray, *Abide in Christ* (Fort Washington, Pennsylvania, 1963), p. 84.

Part II

A Wise Woman's Assignment From God

Chapter One

God's Original Intention

———

And the Lord God said, It is not good that the man
should be alone; I will make him an help meet for him.
And the rib, which the Lord God had taken from man,
made he a woman, and brought her unto the man.
And Adam said, This is now bone of my bones,
and flesh of my flesh.
Genesis 2:18; 22-23

ADAM EXCITEDLY EXCLAIMED

A dam said, "The sky's the limit now – you're everything I ever needed." Eve completed him! Together they would subdue the earth. She was made to be an encourager, a motivator. She was a perfectly suited partner.

I can imagine her saying, "Adam, the names you picked for the animals are splendid. You're brilliant." Or, "Let me help you, Adam! Being here with you is wonderful!" Adam's eyes must have lit up as he was inspired on to another job in God's beautiful garden. He loved Eve and appreciated everything she was and did. It was a perfect relationship.

Then one day the serpent came into the garden. Eve was so naïve and easy to deceive. She didn't even bother to

ask Adam's advice. She thought she remembered what God
had said, but she must have been daydreaming because she
fell for the serpent's line. Sin entered the world, and
trickery and lying were the means Satan used.

Part of Eve's punishment was to have her husband
"lord it over her." Perhaps she then felt oppressed and
misused. She wanted to share more in his accomplishments. Perhaps he didn't ask for her advice because he had
already seen her poor judgment. No doubt she began to nag
and feel sorry for herself. He began to feel unmotivated; the
sky wasn't the limit anymore. Now it was just weeds and
thorns and hard work.

SNARES AND NETS

Years later Solomon was doing some research. He was
looking for someone who sought after wisdom. He had
probably looked high and low for just the right woman, who
would inspire him to fulfill his potential. He observed
hundreds of them with no success. He said, "And I find
more bitter than death the woman, whose heart is snares
and nets, and her hands as bands: whoso pleaseth God
shall escape from her; but the sinner shall be taken by her"
(Ecclesiastes 7:26).

He pictured a woman full of deceit and trickery. She
sought ways to insure her selfish desires. When she caught
her prey, she slipped her hands around his waist and neck.
They became as chains. Her trickery deceived him, but he
was nevertheless bound.

As the years passed some women began to use the
same means as Satan to get their own way. Since they
didn't possess the strength of a man, many times women
resorted to deception. Some women will use any evil means
to accomplish their selfish projects. Jezebel was such a
woman. She sank about as low as a woman can sink. She
misused the office of queen to posses Naboth's vineyard.

She wrote letters in her husband Ahab's name and sealed them with the royal seal. She even gave a spiritual command to proclaim a fast. She arranged for two false witnesses to testify against Ahab resulting in his murder. God's judgment was not immediate, but it was sure. She was a woman whose heart was "snares and nets."

DOES THE END JUSTIFY THE MEANS?

Even many Christian women don't recognize the difference between being creative and being deceptive. The godly woman would not want to use this evil trait. Sometimes, however, she will continue to manipulate others into doing what she considers many "good" projects. She tries to play the Holy Spirit in the lives of her family and friends.

She can't bring herself to trust God to work in the lives of others. Her clever ways are ever before her. She considers herself very righteous and only God Himself can show this woman her heart of "snares and nets and the hands which are as bands."

In the Bible Rebekah illustrates such a woman. She played favorites between her sons. By trickery she went about to accomplish a good thing. Esau, the eldest, despised his birthright which afforded him the right of spiritual leadership. Jacob, her favorite, was interested in spiritual things.

She conceived the scheme to have Jacob, who was a smooth man, imitate his brother Esau, who was a hairy man, to deceive Isaac, their blind father. She put goatskins upon Jacob's hands and neck so that Isaac would mistake Jacob for Esau and give to Jacob Esau's birthright (Genesis 27:16). She probably rationalized to herself that "the end would justify the means." She accomplished what she set out to do, but much heartache was the result because she was a manipulator.

MOTIVATION VS. MANIPULATION

God has endowed the woman with the unique role of motivator. Her husband is called on to be the main decision maker. She can inspire him to greatness. She can motivate him more than any other person through her love and admiration.

There is a fine line between motivation and manipulation. Others may not always be able to discern the difference. The outward acts may be the same – admiring others and doing thoughtful things, but the woman who is a manipulator is doing these things to get her way. She thinks that her way is always best.

The Holy Spirit inwardly motivates the Christian woman to do good works. He provides the inner spark that can be fanned into a flame. How wonderful that God uses human beings as instruments of His motivational power.

If a woman is not controlled by the Holy Spirit, she will probably resort to manipulation. She may subconsciously try to imitate the supernatural force of the Holy Spirit. However, no woman can duplicate this force. How foolish she is to try! The end of manipulation is empty and unfulfilling.

Invite Christ to control your life, and you can become God's inspiring motivator. God will begin changing you into that "perfectly suited" partner to your husband and an inspiration to your children as you ask Him to cleanse your motives and put His will and His glory uppermost in your life.

CHAPTER TWO

A Freedom Demonstration

Blurred Vision

So I'm supposed to be a motivator! If my role as a woman was God's original idea, then I can be excited. It isn't my role that causes the problems; it is sin. Sin causes the abuses and misuses – the thorns and briars in my personal and matrimonial bliss.

Man's spiritual vision can become so blurred that he feels that the woman is inferior. The more sinful he becomes the more he mistreats and enslaves her. After all, he has been created with greater physical strength and with it he can make her comply to his wishes.

Twenty centuries ago Jesus Christ stepped onto the scene. Prejudice against women had become so bad that a man wouldn't even speak to a woman in public. She wasn't allowed the privilege of an education. She had become a sex object, and was considered unworthy to do more than the menial tasks. Yet there were great traces of God's original purpose. Man couldn't do without her. He knew he needed her – even if the reason wasn't clear.

When Jesus died, He freed the woman from her bondage. Galatians 3:28 reveals "There is neither Jew nor

Greek, there is neither bond nor free, there is neither male nor female, for ye are all one in Christ Jesus."

This means that male and female are equal in worth before God. He corrected the abuses that had come through man's sinful nature. He declared that if we wanted to experience the reality of this freedom we must know Him.

> If the Son shall make you free, ye shall be free indeed. (John 8:36)

> Ye shall know the truth, and the truth shall make you free. (John 8:32)

> I am the way, the truth, and the life. (John 14:6)

God's Freedom Demonstration – Jesus Christ

What does this new freedom mean? Are we free to do as we please? Do we even know the true meaning of freedom? Before we attempt to assert our rights for freedom we would do well to study God's concept of freedom. Our freedom is found in Jesus Christ. Shouldn't we look to Him for guidance? He was God's demonstration of freedom. What did He think freedom meant?

God declared His blueprint for revolution that would bring about freedom in the Gospel of John:

> For I came down from heaven, not to do Mine own will, but the will of Him that sent Me. (John 6:38)

> I do nothing of Myself; but as My Father hath taught Me, I speak these things. And He that sent Me is with Me; the Father hath not left Me alone; for I do always those things that please Him. (John 8:28-29)

Woman's Freedom Demonstration

Jesus demonstrated His freedom by doing only what the Father told Him – every moment He was on earth. Isn't this the way we as women should demonstrate our freedom?

Only to be what He wants me to be every moment of every day.

Yielded completely to Jesus alone every step of this pilgrim way.[1]

God's will for women is for us to discover His original intention before sin entered the world. What was the woman's role then? Helper! Partner! Motivator! Modern woman has wanted more than to be freed from the abuses that have resulted from sin. She has wanted to change her God-given role. It is as if she looks up at God and dares to say, "God, I've got a better idea. Let me be the leader half of the time and the man be my helper. Then half of the time he can lead and I'll be the helper. Lord, I'll call it 'egalitarianism.' I think this would be real freedom – real equality."

I Want To Be Leader

There was one long ago who didn't like the role God had given to him, although he was a beautiful creature. He was second in authority to God Himself. But he thought himself far too beautiful and superior to be number two and said, "I will be like the Most High." Satan became the greatest usurper of authority of all time.

The Bible says that a woman is not to teach or usurp authority over the man (1 Timothy 2:12). Many women are saying by their actions, "I'm far too beautiful, far too superior to just be a helper for the man. I will change my role. I will be number one! I know more about what is best for me than God Himself."

Only obedience to God's Word brings true freedom. The truly submissive wife finds that her husband and her God release her to a freedom unknown by others.

Submit to Him, Lord?

Submit to *him*, Lord?
    I'm just as smart as he!
Let *him* be my *head*?
    You're the only head *I* need.

Stay home and clean his house
    and cook his meals?
I have more intelligence than
    to waste my life on such
        lowly things.

It's enough, Lord, that my body
    is the channel to bear his child –
He needs to make it up to me and
    pay someone else to tend my child's
        mundane needs.

My education is lying waste.
    I learned so many things I must
        share to make this world
        a better place.

I'll not be a doormat –
    Help meet *his* needs?
Who'll help meet mine?
    If I stick with this thing
        called marriage
It'll be fifty-fifty or no go!

I have my rights –
    I'm not inferior to any man!
The very least I've earned
    is *equal* rights!

What's that Lord?

You stepped down from glory
    You humbled yourself
Even though You had equal rights
    with God the Father?
You became a servant –
    Even washed your disciples' feet?

You were too good for *that* Lord!

You were obedient unto death
    Even though You were a King?
You let them spit on You, Lord
    Even curse Your holy name?

Why did You do it, Lord?
    Didn't it make You feel inferior?
You submitted to the authority
    of the Father –
You did everything *He* told You to do?
    Submission was the Father's
        plan for *You*?

The reason why You came was not to
    do Your will, but His?
Because You obeyed, the Father did what?
    He *exalted* You?
Gave You a name above every name?

Oh, Lord forgive me!
    I never realized –
I thought to submit meant
    that I was inferior.

You love me just as much as
    You love him?
This is just Your plan for *my life*?
    I don't have to gain equality
        for myself?

If I obey, *You* will lift me up?
    What Lord?
If I'm truly submissive my
    children will rise up and
    call me blessed –
My husband will praise me –
And You, Lord – You will honor me?

Then give me a submissive heart
Oh Lord!
I want to be in your perfect will!

VIVÉ LA DIFFERENCE

Am I then to become nothing? A "yes" person parroting the wishes and opinions of my husband? "Yes, dear!" "That's right, dear!" "Anything you say, dear!" Whoever got the idea that a woman would lose her identity if she was submissive and a helper? Nothing is farther from the truth! No man wants a doormat – a nothing person with no opinions – no distinctives that make her unique.

A woman like that is not a helper but a hindrance. If you were just like him, he would not need you. My husband declares along with the French, "Vivé la difference."

NOTE

1.   Norman Clayton, "Every Moment of Every Day," *Youth Sings* (California: Praise Book Publications © 1938), Song 22.

CHAPTER THREE

THE BATTLE OF IDENTITY

T he feminist movement rages around the identity question. There are many side issues, but "Who am I" seems to be the central factor in the battle. The Christian woman must look at the issue from an entirely different perspective.

SETUP FOR WOMEN'S LIB

Without the Word of God as my authority, I too, would probably be a proponent of "women's lib." I was encouraged in my youth to excel in subjects that were typically male. I didn't take home economics in high school because it was not considered a "worthy" subject for those planning to go to college. I was elected president of mixed groups at various times; I was voted the outstanding senior; I tied with another girl for the second highest grades in our graduating class. Even at church I was encouraged to compete with the young men and beat two young men (now prominent pastors) in a better speakers' tournament.

I don't say this to brag, only to show you that I was a perfect setup for women's lib. It was only the surrounding circumstances in my life and the grace of God that kept me from it.

God's Counterattack

The circumstances that helped counteract my encouragement toward equal authority and leadership roles with men were:

1. A happy home where my father was the head and my mother was submissive.

2. A home where I was encouraged in the home-making arts and where mother made home-making her life's work and was fulfilled by it.

3. A husband who believed that he should be the head of the house.

4. Above all – a belief in the Bible as the infallible Word of God.

I will be forever grateful for the example of my home and for the leadership of my husband, but if it were not for my belief in the Bible I could have easily rationalized and dismissed these as being backward and chauvinistic.

So for years I have stood on the Word of God! I have gone back to the Scriptures time and time again to restudy what they have to say about the woman's place and ministry. I have been tempted many times to take the lead over less capable men, and it has been only God's Word that has kept me from it.

Identity Problems For Christian Women?

Intellectual assent to the Bible, however, does not erase all the problems facing Christian women. Perhaps had it not been for the women's libbers I wouldn't have even recognized that I had a problem. But as they kept crying, "Identity! Identity!" and kept asking, "Who are you, American woman?" I began to slowly peak out from underneath mountains of diapers and endless routine. I had given birth to five babies in eight years. My youngest had just started to school, and I hadn't had time to wonder about "who I was."

I may have been too proud to admit defeat, or it may have been that Christian circles just didn't offer the answers to these problems. Sometimes our meetings are so unrelated to real life that Christian women have to turn to the "world" to find the answers to their problems. Some women just simply work their way through hard times; others just accept them as being a part of "growing up." I don't know which was my problem; I only know that for the first time I began to silently ask, "Who am I, anyway?"

TIME TO BREATHE AGAIN

I began to feel unneeded. I began to reflect on the past when my husband and I had done so many things to serve the Lord together. Those desires began to return. I wanted to become involved in his work again. I had so many "tremendous" ideas on how to improve everything, only now there were full-time male staff members who were responsible for all these details. I began to understand that I was passing through a transitional period of my life. I could not go back to what I had been BC (before children).

If only I had dwelt on "Who I have become," instead of "Who I used to be." I was not the same person anymore. If I had realized that, I could have escaped some of the resentment that inevitably began to form inside of me. I didn't understand myself, and I therefore didn't think anyone else understood me.

A NEW ME

There was a "me" clamoring to burst forth – a new me. I was very similar to that girl of yesterday. You could have recognized many of the same talents and goals, but I was a much better person than I ever could have been BH (before husband) and BC (before children).

Would I go back to living in my little rigid world with everything always planned and everything always organized (never having serendipity because of my rigid organization)?

Would I go back to the unbending standard of perfection I had created for myself (that had created tension problems)?

Would I go back to my shallow Christian life with all my pat answers (but no real compassion for those who sinned and sorrowed)?

Would I go back to my self-righteous list of do's and don'ts (always in bondage and always trying to please others instead of God)?

Would I go back to a life of doing things for God (instead of letting God do things through me with Him getting the glory)?

Would I go back to hiding from my inadequacies and fears (instead of facing them in faith and having the joy of overcoming)?

No, no – a thousand times no!

Ms. Or Mrs.?

God has used my husband, my children, and the circumstances of life to make me into "another" Joyce. I used to "be happy"; now my life is one of truly rejoicing. I'm thrilled to be Mrs. Adrian Rogers. Others can use Ms. if they want to. I'm very happy being the person I am.

I need my husband. He thinks the things that I think are impossible are possible. Because of his positive spirit I have been overseas ten times. Because of his positive spirit I have learned that I can try innovative projects. Throughout our marriage, all the really worthwhile things that I have done have been done only because of the support and encouragement of my husband and children. They have been God's chief tools in pruning me and bringing forth spiritual fruit in my life. Were it not for them, you wouldn't be reading this book!

WITHOUT THEM

Without them I would have thought I was adequate, independent, and self-sufficient. I would have tried to do something spectacular with my life in order to become somebody.

Without them I wouldn't have known what true fulfillment as a woman was. I would never have known the fulfillment that love and dependence brings.

Even the "little one" who was snatched from his crib by death – without him in my life (even if but for a little while), I would never have known the deep comfort of God's Holy Spirit and the deep inadequacy of not being able to help myself – therefore learning for the first time total dependence on God. I wouldn't have learned the priceless lesson of how to comfort those who grieve.

I am proud to be Mrs. Adrian Rogers, wife and mother of four wonderful children. You could never know "who I am" without knowing these special people God has placed in my life. Jack Taylor said it best, "They [family] are God's perfect gifts to me to help in perfecting me."[1] I am proud to be a part of them, and I am proud of them to be a part of me.

BELIEVING GOD TO CORRECT MISTAKES AND ABUSES

As long as men and women are in human bodies they will be prone to mistakes. Christian men and women are not exceptions to the rule. They just know how to begin again when mistakes are made.

God knew that men would make mistakes and sometimes even be abusive. How can a woman help to correct these errors without becoming a rebellious nag?

1. She must be filled with the Holy Spirit, thereby manifesting a joyful, thankful heart (see Ephesians 5:18-20).

2. She must not neglect her outward appearance, but her primary concern should be on the inner qualities of a meek and quiet spirit. This means that she should be both inwardly and outwardly submissive (see Ephesians 5:33).

3. She should pray for her husband (and other male leadership), asking God to point out their weak points to them (see Ephesians 6:18).

4. She should lovingly entreat her husband in very creative ways where she feels it is appropriate. Great wisdom is needed to discern the difference between entreating and nagging (see Proverbs 27:15).

5. She should then trust God to bring pressure to bear on that male authority in her life, expecting God and not the man to work a miracle (see Hebrews 13:18).

Do you really think you can do a better job than God? Obedience at each of the preceding levels makes it possible to believe God for the results.

I GOTTA BE ME – IN CHRIST

Something within me cries out against being a "rubber-stamped copy." With the songwriter I say, "I gotta be me." But as a Christian I have to modify that to say, "I gotta be me – in Christ." I can never find fulfillment in doing exactly as I please. My self-centered actions must be surrendered to Christ.

I began my Christian life with the discovery that Christ died for my sins (see Rom. 5:8). It wasn't until later that I became aware of the fact that I was "crucified with

Christ" (Galatians 2:20). My old sinful self died that day two thousand years ago. I can count on that fact. My focus now should be on living unto God. "I am crucified with Christ; nevertheless I live; yet not I, but Christ liveth in me" (Galatians 2:20).

I am no longer the person I used to be. I am now a new creature. I must discover that new person that I am and yield unto God. As hard as it may be to see, God is fashioning a masterpiece out of my life.

His Masterpiece

God said of me, His child,
  "You are My workmanship,
    My poem, My masterpiece."
Not that I gave outward evidence
  of such prospect,
But God saw in me a destiny.
I was like a stone in the heap,
  broken and useless,
But God passed by.

He saw me lying there in the dust.
  He stopped to pick me up.
He held me in His hand.
    By His grace that day
    He brushed away the dust
    And began His masterpiece.

IT FITS ME TO A "T"

In understanding that unique "me" I must consider at least six areas:
1. Temperament
2. Training
3. Talents
4. Treasures
5. Tasks
6. Time

TEMPERAMENT

According to Tim LaHaye there are four basic temperaments. They are discussed at length in his book, *The Spirit-Controlled Temperament*.[2] The sanguine and the choleric temperaments are the more outgoing personalities, while the melancholy and the phlegmatic temperaments are the more introverted ones. The sanguine is the bubbly, energetic, "life of the party." The choleric is the dominant, aggressive leader. The melancholy is the gifted, sensitive, and sometimes moody individual. And the phlegmatic is the one who always seems to be calm, cool, and collected. Each person has one dominant temperament rounded out and complimented by any unique combination of the other three.

Each temperament has both strengths and weaknesses. For every strength I need to realize that without Him I can do nothing (see John 15:5). But the really exciting discovery is that the Holy Spirit has strength for every weakness. "I can do all things through Christ which strengtheneth me" (Philippians 4:13).

God designed me in a special way in order for me to meet special needs. No one else can fill my shoes!

TRAINING

I need to take a look at my background. What kind of family did I come from?

❖   Formal or informal
❖   Christian or non-Christian
❖   Loving or cold

What type of education did I receive?

❖   High school
❖   College
❖   Graduate school

What kind of experiences have I had?

- ❖ Traveled or stayed at home
- ❖ Sports-minded or studious
- ❖ Lived in the country or the city

I'm not responsible for some of these factors. God placed me in a particular family, with certain financial advantages or disadvantages. I was raised either in a small town or a big city. It wasn't until I grew older that I was able to make choices for myself. I should not, however, despise any of my background experiences, for God has put them in my life in order to enable me to minister more effectively to others.

TALENTS

In my "positive probe" I must examine carefully my potential talents:

- ❖ Ability to create art
- ❖ Ability to perform musically
- ❖ Ability to speak
- ❖ Ability to write
- ❖ Ability to teach
- ❖ Ability to care for children
- ❖ Ability to sew
- ❖ Ability to cook
- ❖ Ability to listen

The sooner I discover my talents, the sooner I can develop them. God will not miraculously supply me with abilities that can be gained through practice and hard work. I must make an effort to receive training.

If you are a multi-talented person, ask the Lord to help you choose which talents to develop to their fullest. Otherwise you will become a "Jill-of-all-trades and master of none." Many "gifted" persons are living frustrated lives because of their own indecision and lack of direction.

Find one talent that you would like to have as your
focal point. Let the other talents become a beautiful
backdrop across your life. They will add richness and
diversity. Perhaps even in later years you will find time to
develop them.

TREASURES

On top of a Christian woman's natural talents she also
possesses supernatural gifts. They are spiritual treasures to
be discovered. God gives each Christian at least one
spiritual gift. The various gifts are described in 1
Corinthians 12 and 14 and Romans 12. You should pray
and ask the Lord to reveal to you what your gift or gifts
are.

Once discovered, the gift should be developed to its
highest potential. You can do this by being continually
filled with the Holy Spirit and by receiving training in
areas of ministry where you could effectively use your gift.

I believe that God matches these spiritual treasures to
your natural talents and temperaments. For instance, a
person with the talent for singing may have the gift of
exhortation. If so, she then has a supernatural ability to
comfort and build others up in the faith through her
singing. Someone else with the gift of mercy might express
that gift through the talent of caring for children. A woman
with the gift of prophecy could exercise her gift through
the talent of writing.

There are endless combinations of talents and gifts.
This is because you are a unique individual through whom
God wishes to minister to a needy world.

TASKS

I need to understand that my task or role as a woman
is constantly changing. In my lifetime I may wear several

different "hats" – wife, mother, teacher, pastor's wife. Adjustments to my tasks were constantly required as my children grew from babies to teenagers. More adjustments were required as I made the change from mother-in-law to grandmother. Some women experience subtraction from their roles – they are widows. All of these factors greatly affect my everyday living. Joyful acceptance of whatever the task is for me from year to year is one of the secrets of fulfillment.

TIME OF LIFE

The time of life I am in is very closely related to my tasks. Jill Renich lists these phases as:

Childhood, learning (educational) phase, childbearing years, ministry (after forty) – the peak of a woman's life when she's basically over the learning-mistakes era and is able to forge ahead with the wisdom acquired in earlier years yet with the vitality of the middle years, and the maturity, mellowness, and added wisdom of the older years.

As I progress from one phase of my life to another, my life changes. It has been enlarged by the circumstances that have surrounded it.

GROWING PAINS

Just as teenagers experience some "growing pains" when they come through adolescence, so you can expect to experience the same type things when you go through transitional years.

Extra time and understanding may be needed when you realize that all your children have grown up. You will need to rediscover who you really are. On the other hand if you have no children, you may need something "extra" to fill the void in your life and provide you with fulfillment.

By nature a woman is ordinarily more emotional than a man. We must take care of ourselves both physically and spiritually in order to make it through these phases of our lives. We must lean on the Lord for our emotional stability. Each phase of life offers its unique joys. You can learn to have the time of your life each day of your life.

NOTES

1. Jack Taylor, *One Home Under God* (Nashville, Tennessee: Broadman Press, 1974), p. 109.
2. Tim LaHaye, *The Spirit-Controlled Temperament* (Wheaton, Illinois: Tyndale House Publishers, 1966).

CHAPTER FOUR

GOD'S SPECIAL COMMAND

—◆—

There are many commands given to all Christians, but to women God has given one very special command. In Titus, the second chapter, verse 5, God says that women are to be "keepers at home." The portrait of the virtuous woman found in Proverbs 31:27 reveals that, "She looketh well to the ways of her household." Paul says in 1 Timothy 5:14, "I will therefore that the younger women marry, bear children, guide the house, give none occasion to the adversary to speak reproachfully."

The traditional male-female roles are being challenged today. There is much confusion and extremism on both sides of the issue. Some want to completely discard the idea of roles. Childbearing and physical strength put a kink in this line of thinking. Extremists compensate for the "inequities" of life by proposing child-care centers, inexpensive birth control measures, and legislation for equal job opportunities and pay.

The other extremist group tries to limit the woman's sphere of activity to the home alone, totally ignoring the fact that scientific advancements have made it possible for her to complete her household duties in much less time.

God would like for us to have a balanced view somewhere between the two extremes. The wise woman will
look at these issues from God's point of view.

THE PRIORITY OF HOMEMAKING

> Homemaking is the most satisfying and most rewarding of all
> careers (for women). This is the way God planned it to be.[1]

If you have chosen marriage, you have already chosen
to be a homemaker. Homemaking must always be your
first priority. Another career or various side projects can
never again be first in your life.

This does not mean that it will have to consume all
your time. How time-consuming homemaking is will vary
with the number and ages of your children, the desires of
your husband, your physical strength, and your temperament type. There will be time for extra hobbies and side
projects, but never as your first priority.

AN ATTITUDE OF CONTENTMENT

The fulfillment you gain from homemaking will
depend on your attitude. It must be an attitude of contentment. The word content comes from a Latin word
meaning "to hold together."

> When you are content your thoughts are holding together in
> the situation you find yourself. You think clearly. You keep in
> focus true values of life. As a natural result, you think, talk,
> and act in an organized manner.[2]

If you aren't content, you are doubting God's wonderful provisions for your happiness. The psalmist expressed
it this way: "In the multitude of my thoughts within me
Thy comforts delight my soul" (Psalm 94:19).

You should be content not only with how God made
you, but also with the circumstances in your life that you

cannot change. Perhaps the greatest cause for marital unhappiness is discontentment. Some people are always searching for more. You think that you will be happy with

❖ That new husband   ❖ A new baby
❖ A new car   ❖ A new house
❖ A second baby   ❖ A better job
❖ A second car   ❖ A bigger house
              ❖ And on and on!

Kate complained about her house until Bob bought her a new one. Then he took on two jobs to meet the payments. He was never home it seemed. Soon she began accusing him of not caring for them. She made the few hours he was at home so miserable for him that he was glad to leave again. Instead of changing her attitude, she blamed him for her unhappiness. Within two years she married the fellow next door.[3]

CONTENTMENT IS LEARNED

Contentment doesn't come naturally. Paul said, "I have learned, in whatsoever state I am, therewith to be content" (Philippians 4:11). This learning process involves counting your blessings and focusing on the things that you *do* like instead of on the things that you *don't* like.

When my husband accepted the pastorate at Bellevue Baptist Church, we moved from Florida to Tennessee. Some folks think that Tennessee is in the deep South, but as far as I was concerned it was about as north as could be. It was rainy and cold. Memphis seemed enormous. But I took that Scripture literally, "in whatsoever state I am." That had to mean Florida or Tennessee. I chose to be content in Tennessee. And I was! The Lord added so many extra blessings to my life that I never would have recognized had I not chosen contentment.

GRATITUDE, THE FOUNDATION OF CONTENTMENT

The fall is thrilling to me with its magnificent changing of the leaves. Then after the bleak, cold winter comes the wonder of springtime. I often praise Him for allowing me to be a part of these visible miracles. I had never experienced these in Florida. It has been said that some people always see the glass half empty, while others see it half full. Ella May Miller says, "Gratitude is the foundation upon which contentment is built."

SEEING GOD IN THE ORDINARY

Truly there are blessings all around you. Christ is all in all. His fingerprints are all over His creation. It is not difficult to marvel at a glorious sunset or stand amazed at the ocean's edge, where you can gaze as far as your naked eye can see, and watch those powerful billows roar to a silent stop on the shore. Surely, only God could engineer such a feat.

When spring is abloom with its magnificent array of flowers – pink and white, yellow and purple – your heart consciously calls out to this God of exquisite beauty.

But do you see God in the ordinary? Often outside the window of my study, I see birds and squirrels feeding on the seed I've sprinkled there. They all look so very ordinary. Yet I've learned to leave my binoculars nearby. When I concentrate on one of these so-called "dull" little creatures, a world of hidden beauty bursts forth. Delicate colors – shades of gray and brown and rust – black markings, white collars and even bright yellow spots appear when viewed this way. Each of these creatures has markings so delicate and so unique.

The world of the "ordinary" is really not so ordinary with God. He has put as much effort in their creation as the more flamboyant cardinal and blue jay. It is all waiting there for the one who will take the time and effort to see with more than just the naked eye.

THANK YOU, JESUS

The loving expression of a thoughtful God is everywhere. If I can only learn to say, "Thank you, Jesus for all You have done," He will fill me with inner peace and joy. In Christ I can find the strength to change my wrong attitudes. He can help me organize my thoughts. God cares about my every-day frustrations.

IN CHRIST ALL THINGS CONSIST

He is holding everything together. Won't you hand your life over to Him? Without him you will "come apart."

But godliness with contentment is great gain....And having food and raiment let us be therewith content. (1 Timothy 6:6,8)

Let your conversation be without covetousness, and be content with such things as ye have; for He hath said, I will never leave thee, nor forsake thee. (Hebrews 13:5)

THE DIGNITY OF DRUDGERY

One thing that robs the homemaker of her contentment is the drudgery of her life. Many feel like the daily chores are so boring and unchallenging. They think that if they could only rid themselves of the "drudgery," life would be satisfying.

Don't forget what God said to Adam and Eve in the Garden of Eden after sin entered their lives. He declared, "Cursed is the ground for thy sake" (Genesis 3:17). You may not understand why, but God intended to use the drudgery to work out His will in our lives.

Work comes hand in hand with homemaking – hard work! Nothing worthwhile is ever achieved without drudgery. There is no debut of the concert pianist without years of endless "drudgery" at scales and finger exercises. There is no successful heart transplant without the years of study and hard routine.

It is by means of drudgery that the spectacular is attained. But don't live for the spectacular. Let God tend to that. Don't despise the endless household chores:

1. Three meals a day;
2. Mountains of diapers to fold;
3. Endless fingerprints on the windows and doors;
4. Constant crumbs on the floor.

For our sakes God takes the so-called drudgery and runs it straight through our lives as a means of bringing into unity once again the "dust" and the "divine." You can make a "little bit of heaven" out of your earthly home if you will learn to accept God's means of perfecting your life. He can transform your drudgery into joy with His presence.

Beatitudes for Homemakers

BLESSED is she whose daily tasks are a work of love; for her willing hands and happy heart transform duty into joyous service to all her family and God.

BLESSED is she who opens the door to welcome both stranger and well-loved friend; for gracious hospitality is a test of brotherly love.

BLESSED is she who mends stockings and toys and broken hearts; for her understanding is a balm to her husband and children.

BLESSED is she who scours and scrubs; for well she knows that cleanliness is one expression of godliness.

BLESSED is she whom children love; for the love of a child is of greater value than fortune or fame.

BLESSED is she who sings at her work; for music lightens the heaviest load and brightens the dullest chore.

BLESSED is she who dusts away doubt and fear and sweeps out the cobwebs of confusion; for her faith will triumph over all adversity.

BLESSED is she who serves laughter and smiles with every meal; for her cheerfulness is an aid to mental and physical digestion.

BLESSED is she who introduces Jesus Christ to her children; for godly sons and daughters shall be her reward.

BLESSED is she who preserves the sacredness of the Christian home; for hers is a divine trust that crowns her with dignity.[4]

–Adapted by Ella May Miller

NOTES

1. Ella May Miller, *A Woman in Her Home* (Chicago: Moody Press, 1968), p. 13. Used by permission.
2. Ella May Miller, *Contentment – Great Gain* (Virginia: Heart to Heart), pamphlet. Used by permission.
3. Ibid.
4. Ella May Miller, *A Woman in Her Home*, p. 14.

Part III

A WISE WOMAN'S ACHIEVEMENTS THROUGH GOD

CHAPTER ONE

CREATIVE HOMEMAKING

———

I don't want to be an ordinary housewife, getting by with as little effort as possible. I want my home to be more than just a place to come for meals and a bed in which to sleep. I want to live creatively even in the ordinary circumstances of life.

SETTING GOALS

A wise homemaker sets challenging goals for herself. Her husband and her children will be uppermost in these objectives. Before you read on, sit down with pen and paper in hand and verbalize your own inner goals. I did this and arrived at these over-arching goals:

1. For all my family to love and serve Jesus Christ.

2. To be content with the possessions I have and the circumstances of my life.

3. For my husband to be working at a job for which he is best suited and one in which he can best glorify God, regardless of monetary gain.

4. To provide a creative home atmosphere where the family can enjoy being together and sharing hospitality with their friends.

5.   To care adequately for my family's physical needs.

6.   To provide whatever education, training, and encouragement is needed to equip my children for a contented life.

7.   To spend enough time with my husband and family for us all to enjoy the blessings of love and fellowship.

8.   To use my gifts and talents in a meaningful way.

There can be a variety of outward means to accomplish your goals. You should work out short-range ways to reach these long-range goals. Aiding your children and husband to set their goals can also be one of the greatest contributions you can make as a wife and mother. This will take time – a lot of time. But if your goals are worthwhile, it will be worth any sacrifice you make.

When you are setting your goals for your family, don't forget to set some personal goals for yourself. Always have a challenging project that you are working on. Use that education if you have been privileged to receive one. Don't be tricked into thinking that you will waste your education if you don't have a paid job outside of the home.

> Education of women is fine, but why not also teach them how to use their knowledge and skill in the home setting? The educated mother can better answer the hundreds of daily questions. She can interpret life more intelligently. She can better follow her children in their school and community activities. She can use her knowledge of science, of mathematics, her artistic and nursing skills, within the framework of her home. Education can help produce better wives and mothers if used in the proper way.[1]

CREATING AN ATMOSPHERE

> Speaking to yourselves in psalms and hymns and spiritual songs, singing and making melody in your heart to the Lord! (Ephesians 5:19)

songs, singing and making melody in your heart to the Lord! (Ephesians 5:19)

Creative homemaking is so much more than merely providing for the necessities of life. It is all wrapped up in the atmosphere that you create. The atmosphere is dependent upon your own personal attitude. Are you a happy person who is singing as you work? Are you pleasant and courteous with your husband and your children?

Music is one of the best ways to create a joyful atmosphere. Christian records and tapes can be played around the home, starting when the children are very young. The hymnbook should be given a prominent place. Any interest in music can be encouraged in family members.

You can fill the hearts and minds of your children with challenging Christian books which will give them a burning desire to do God's will for their lives.

You can increase your children's Bible knowledge by purchasing Christian coloring books, puzzles, and games. Family worship can be made both fun and challenging by playing games such as Bible baseball, or by having a Bible drill among the children. When my children were growing up, I placed Scripture cards at their dinner plates for them to read aloud before we ate.

When your children get older they can take turns leading the family devotions. Prayer requests of common interests should be shared by the entire family. Each child should be encouraged to have a personal time of devotions and Scripture memory.

With imagination you can create an atmosphere of faith in which Scripture can be applied to day-by-day experiences. Disappointments can be faced later on in life if you have taught your children an attitude of praise and thanksgiving.

But by far the most important atmosphere that you set for your children is an atmosphere of love. This is taught more by example than by words, but don't underestimate the necessity for words. Learn to say, "I love you" often.

FAMILY TRADITIONS

Holidays, birthdays, and graduations can all be meaningful times to draw the family closer together. They should be remembered and treasured. While our children were living at home we inaugurated many family traditions.

On birthdays and graduations at our house the children came to expect a display of pictures and handiwork done by them at various ages. Their individual accomplishments were recognized and pictures were taken.

On Thanksgiving, members of the family came to the dinner table ready to name a specific thing for which they would like to thank the Lord. As they shared the event or person for which they were thankful, they lit a candle on the Thanksgiving wreath, which was the centerpiece for the table.

The story of the birth of Jesus was, and continues to be, a part of our Christmas celebration. As gifts are opened, something special is featured. One year verses about giving were placed on the presents; another time a good wish for the next year was given from one family member to another; another time verses from Isaiah, prophesying about Jesus, the Messiah, were read. An open Bible and the manger scene are central in the decorations.

Our family took part in special Christmas church services. Our children were encouraged to give a Christmas offering for foreign missions. Each year we tried to visit shut-ins and give something special to someone in need. All were encouraged to invite their friends to enjoy the hospitality of our home.

One Easter small objects that symbolized the crucifixion and resurrection stories were placed at each place on the table. Each person showed his object, told what it represented, then read the Scripture that was attached. Examples of the objects were part of a sponge, three nails, a wooden cross, a stone, an angel, and a piece of white cloth.

Mother's and Father's Day always brought a special time for each of the children to tell why they were thankful for their parents.

Each day can also be a time of celebration and honor for different members of the family. Each family member had a name plaque with his or her name on it, along with its Christian meaning and an applicable Bible verse. These plaques were alternated every morning and placed on the breakfast table. The person whose plaque was on the table became the "person for the day," and was prayed for in a special way that day. These plaques also served as a vital part of the decorations during the birthday and graduation festivities.

Home Décor – An Expression Of Faith

A home should not be decorated pretentiously, to impress other people. It should be designed to be lived in and enjoyed. The décor should express not only your personality and your tastes, but also your faith in Christ. Somewhere there should be expressions that show you know and love our Lord. This doesn't mean that you have to have a big picture of Jesus hanging in the living room. The way you express yourselves will be as different as your varying personalities.

My home has a large family Bible on a stand in our living room. On the open pages of the Bible we have placed a crown of thorns. Around the room, worked into our decorations are various treasures collected on a number of trips to the Holy Land. These include an olivewood shepherd with his sheep, a rock from the hill of Calvary, a carving of the two spies returning from Canaan, and pictures of the Holy Land on the walls. Scripture texts are also displayed at our front entrance and throughout the house. And Christian books are on the shelves.

We have many other items in our decorations, such as paintings of outdoor scenes, flower arrangements, family pictures and ginger jars. Our colors express our favorites, green and gold, orange and brown. We love the outdoors, so our house has lots of glass so that we can see our backyard and neighborhood lake.

Our home isn't filled with expensive items, but I love it. It reminds me of so many lovely memories. Best of all, you can tell that a Christian family lives there.

Notes

1.   Ella May Miller, *A Woman in Her Home* (Chicago: Moody Press, 1968), p. 67.

CHAPTER TWO

NATURALLY NUTRITIOUS

———◆———

*She looketh well to the ways of her household
and eateth not the bread of idleness.*
Proverbs 31:27

A wise woman will prepare nutritious and appealing
meals. These, of course, will include the six nutrients:
1) protein, 2) carbohydrates, 3) fats, 4) vitamins, 5) minerals, and 6) water.

> They are present in the foods we eat and contain chemical
> substances that function in one or more of three ways: they
> furnish the body with heat and energy, they provide material for
> growth and repair of body tissues, and they assist in the regula-
> tion of body processes.[1]

In the beginning God provided "naturally nutritious"
foods. Big industrial food processors have refined, substi-
tuted, and artificially preserved these products. Most of us
are uninformed. We blindly trust the government to make
sure that industry uses nutritious ingredients.

The producer knows that if he keeps food in its natural
state that it will spoil within a short time. Therefore, he
adds preservatives to his product. Shelf life benefits the food

industry and our convenience-prone laziness. For years we have thought that the chemicals being added to our food to preserve it were harmless; however, many harmful results have been surfacing in recent years.

Some of the means of preservation are being labeled as cancer-causing. Other means just simply rob the food of its nutritional value. Some people don't care. They had rather die a few years sooner than give up their convenience foods. Others are oblivious to the whole process.

Don't fall prey to these invisible thieves and silent killers. Whether you understand God's laws or not, they will still operate the way God intended. One of these laws is that correct eating habits promote good health. You must take it upon yourself to obtain an education and become aware of the positive and negative aspects of nutrition.

The Bible isn't a nutritional textbook, but you may be surprised when you find out that it is filled with nutritional admonitions. Although not necessary to our salvation, the dietary guidelines given to Israel provide material for thought. God wants you to eat correctly.

NUTRITIONAL CONVERSION

> Know ye not that your body is the temple of the Holy Ghost. (1 Corinthians 6:19)

Before you begin to revamp your eating habits you should have a "conversion" experience. You must become convicted that you have been eating incorrectly. You need to make a drastic change in the attitudes that have been deeply ingrained since childhood. As with every area of your life, Christ is the only One who can give you both the desire and the power to change your appetite. Until you are willing to let Christ have control of this area, until you are converted to nutritious eating, you will never be able to change.

Several years ago a friend, Terri Nanney, shared with me about the changed health she had experienced through proper nutrition. I re-examined our family's eating habits. For years I thought that I had been preparing nutritious meals, only to discover that I had fallen into poor nutritional habits without even realizing it.

Deceitful Dainties vs. Nutritious Nibblers

Put a knife to thy throat, if thou be a man given to appetite. Be not desirous of his dainties: for they are deceitful meat. (Proverbs 23:2-3).

I found out that many of my snack foods were almost totally devoid of any nutritional value. Out of my ignorance they had become a regular part of my daily fare. My grocery list included:

* Regular and diet cold drinks
* Cookies
* Crackers
* Pop Tarts
* Sweet rolls and donuts
* Little chocolate cakes with pink icing (they looked and tasted so yummy)

These modern nutritional disasters could probably be classified with what the Bible calls "deceitful dainties." There are many "nutritious nibblers." They should be available at all times. The following are delicious:

* Mixed nuts
* Dried fruit
* Peanut butter and honey on whole wheat bread
* Hot whole wheat bread
* Nutritious cookies
* Bran or carrot muffins
* Pumpkin, banana, or zucchini bread
* Fresh fruit

Refined Foods

One of the chief causes of American nutritional robbery is the refining process. Refined products include white sugar, white flour, white rice, and common table salt. For many years I ignorantly thought that I needed these products. I've learned through study that I don't need refined foods at all. Every nutrient and food that I need can and should be supplied through natural sources.

Refined foods are dead foods. They only provide empty calories. Vitamins, trace minerals, and fiber have all been removed. The long-accepted theory that "a carbohydrate is a carbohydrate is a carbohydrate" is just not so. There is a tremendous difference between the life-giving natural carbohydrates and the death-giving, man-refined carbohydrates.

A diet filled with fresh vegetables and fruits, dairy products, non-fatty meat (not excessive), legumes, natural oil, and whole grains is what God intended us to eat.

Moderation or self-control is a fruit of the Spirit. Too many modern Christians are gluttonous eaters and are not a good testimony for Christ. They aren't keeping their bodies as fit temples for the Holy Spirit.

A Word Of Personal Testimony

Several years ago I committed myself to a healthier way of eating. This has involved eliminating some items from my diet, adding other items to it, and becoming more conscientious in the buying and preparation of foods.

It has been hard work to "reprogram" lifelong habits and to correct convenience-prone attitudes. It has now become a natural part of my life, and it has been well worth every bit of time and energy I have invested.

My main purpose has been to make my body a healthier temple for the Holy Spirit to live in.

I've become convinced that every homemaker should become an expert in the field of nutrition. To my surprise, most have only a surface knowledge of the subject and are influenced mainly by advertisements and hearsay.

Since changing my eating habits, I've experienced a much greater vitality. I challenge you to search for the truth in this area and then work it out in your own life.

How To Get Started

I started the wrong way. Overnight I threw out all of the junk food in the house. I wouldn't recommend this unless you live by yourself and are very disciplined. It will be much easier on everyone if you work into this new way of eating gradually.

Having made some mistakes, I feel like I could make some suggestions that would be of benefit. I think it would be best to work in two stages. Learn the truths and work them out of your own life before you go on to anything else. Don't get discouraged; you have an entire lifetime of bad eating habits to overcome.

Stage One. a) have fresh fruit available at all times; b) cook with as many fresh vegetables as possible; c) cut down on junk foods, especially carbonated and caffeine drinks; d) fix a nutritious breakfast consisting of high-protein foods, whole grains, and fruit; e) begin reading labels for harmful preservatives and refined ingredients.

Stage Two. Purchase basic unrefined food items which are also free from harmful preservatives: a) whole wheat flour, b) brown rice, c) cold-pressed oil (I recommend safflower oil, the lowest in saturated fat), and d) raw, local honey.

To work these items into everyday use begin doing these things:

1. Stop the use of bleached, so-called "enriched" white flour. Begin by cooking with unbleached white flour with wheat germ added.

2.   Then use one-half unbleached white flour and one-half whole-wheat flour. Finally, use all whole wheat flour, except for special occasions.

3.   Begin frying or cooking with oil instead of hydrogenated shortening. Don't use any animal fat.

4.   Begin substituting honey for sugar. Place honey on the table every meal that jelly or syrup is used. Substitute first in items in which the taste can't be detected. Examples are custard, pumpkin pie, carrot muffins, honey oatmeal cake, and banana-nut bread.

I realize there are many controversial opinions about nutrition. I don't claim to be an expert, and I have written briefly about a complex topic. Some resource books are listed in the bibliography on which I have based my conclusions.

As in all areas of life, you must examine various opinions, then choose for yourself. I hope you will remember that your "body is the temple of the Holy Spirit" and will choose those foods that are "naturally nutritious."

Note

1.   *Nutrition Almanac* (New York: McGraw-Hill Book Co., 1975), p. 11.

CHAPTER THREE

GROWING UP TOGETHER

———◆———

The secret of a love that continues to flourish after marriage is the same thing that kept my husband and me together from grammar school to the present time. It is a love that continues to grow. One year I bought my husband a little figurine valentine that said, "Loving you is what I do best." I want this to be one of my greatest achievements. It's so easy to slide into a dull humdrum routine, maintaining a status quo. Yesterday's courtesy and charm won't suffice for today.

This growth needs to be balanced in all three areas of our lives – the spiritual, psychological, and physical.

SPIRITUAL GROWTH

Christ wants us to "grow up into Him" together. Although we may be very different in our temperaments, our basic beliefs and goals must be the same if we are going to grow together. To begin with we should date and marry someone who is at a similar stage of spiritual growth. Then the partner's earnest desire for the future should be "to be like Jesus."

We should feel comfortable praying with each other, discussing spiritual things, and serving the Lord together.

Christian friends and church activities will be some of the means in our spiritual growth. But the home is the chief laboratory for learning. At home we have stripped off our façade, enabling us to recognize more clearly our growth as well as our failures.

Our love will be richer if we are able to share our deepest spiritual desires with our partner. As we grow together in Christ we will be able to help one another more and more.

Help Or Harshness

We will need to learn to temper our "help" with love so that our partner will recognize it as help instead of harshness. There is no better guide to what love is all about than 1 Corinthians 13. Here is a teenage version of that Scripture:

If You Don't Have Love

You can read your Bible every single day,
    You can talk to God for hours and mean
        every word you say.
You can prophesy the future, tell the
    things that are gonna be.
You can have great understanding, reveal
    all kinds of mystery.

But if you don't have love, you don't
    have nothing at all.
You better think about it, you just can't
    live without it.

You can give God all your money, 'til
    You don't have nothing more;
You can sell all your possessions, give
    it all to feed the poor.
You can keep the Ten Commandments, follow
    the Golden Rule,

You can go to church on Sunday, have
    everybody fooled.

Love is always patient,
    Love is always kind;
Love never wants its own way,
    Never speaks its mind;
Love is never jealous,
    Never thinks about itself,
Only wants to know what it
    can do for someone else.

You can give God all your money, 'til
    you don't have nothing more;
You can sell all your possessions,
    give it all to feed the poor;
You can have faith to move a mountain,
    make it crumble into sand;
You can speak to God in languages
    that no one can understand.

But if you don't have love,
    You don't have nothing at all;
You better think about it,
    You just can't live without it!

                         – Steve Rogers

PSYCHOLOGICAL GROWTH

The second part of this relationship is psychological. The truly smart woman will never pit her intelligence or wit against the man she loves. There are many areas where she can excel without "locking horns" with him. An underlying principle for a successful marriage is "don't compete with your partner – but complete your partner."

The greatest Christian women I know have a gentle reticence when in their husband's presence. They are genuine helpmeets. They are talented and gifted, but they exercise these talents and gifts in a wise way – never in competition with their husbands. Doing this will release your husband to admire and encourage you. Don't, however, carry this to an extreme. Never be so uninformed that you aren't interesting to talk with. Keep abreast of the major current events.

Learning to communicate effectively your dreams and your desires along with your fears and your dislikes is a skillful art. You must grow in this ability. To allow someone to see you as you really are is a frightening experience. You long for approval, encouragement, and admiration. Careless and damaging remarks about your partner's inner thoughts can cause a lifetime of wounded feelings. But you can also learn from your mistakes. Forgiveness is the watchword for a successful marriage. For every effort of forgiveness a marriage grows by leaps and bounds.

PHYSICAL GROWTH

There is a unique fulfillment in the sexual realm of marriage. One woman, one man, one flesh was God's idea. Ironically enough, this sexual fulfillment never precludes acceptance and enjoyment of the unique individuality of the other person. Only then can the physical relationship become a genuine expression of true love and care of the other person.

Sexual enjoyment and loving expressions will increase in meaning and satisfaction as you grow in every area of your marriage. There must be a balance between inner and outer beauty. You must constantly be aware of cleanliness and good grooming. Neglect in these areas will diminish the degree of physical satisfaction. There are, however, many beautiful women who have lost their husbands to someone far less attractive.

Nagging, criticism, and a sour, bitter spirit can kill physical enjoyment. On the other hand, nothing will enhance it more than admiration and encouragement.

How's Your Love Life?

There are a lot of misconceptions about sex. Extremism on both sides exists. Some think that if you keep sex on your mind all day long then greater satisfaction can be reached at night. Others give sex very little thought – they only tolerate it for the other benefits of the home.

If a happy medium can be reached much joy will be found. A woman can certainly be creative in her love life. A friend of mine wisely said, "If you are serving T-bone steak at home, your husband won't want bologna somewhere else." Satisfaction in this area of your marriage also increases as each learns the needs and desires of the other. Each needs to grow in his or her ability to communicate about the physical side of marriage. Continue to grow in knowledge. There are a number of good Christian books on this act of marriage. God intended husband and wife to enjoy one another.

CHAPTER FOUR

A QUIVER FULL

—◆—

Lo, children are an heritage of the Lord:
and the fruit of the womb is His reward.
As arrows are in the hand of a mighty man;
so are children of the youth.
Happy is the man that hath his quiver full of them.
Psalm 127:3-5

For the majority of women, building a home naturally includes children. Not until modern methods of birth control came about did women even begin to question that motherhood was a part of marriage. Those who were barren were often an object of pity.

Both the population explosion and extreme women's movements have cast doubts on the wisdom of having children – especially, of all things, "a quiver full of them."

You shouldn't look to this generation with its multiplicity of hang-ups to provide the answer to this dilemma. The wise woman will look to the Bible for her guidance. Psalm 127 provides a principle for her to go by. It says that the man who has his "quiver" full of children will be happy. One of God's rewards is children. The Bible does not say

in any place how many a quiver full is. You must seek
God's guidance to show you how many this is for you.

From examining this Scripture you can see that raising
children is supposed to be a rewarding experience. It is
supposed to bring joy and fulfillment. God has put a
vacuum into a woman that cannot be fulfilled outside of
motherhood. God intended for the Spirit-controlled
woman to "work out her salvation" through the career of
motherhood (see 1 Timothy 2:15).

To the woman who is unable to have children, or the
woman who chooses to remain unmarried, I believe God
provides avenues of nurturing "spiritual children." God
cares for those women who are unmarried and barren. He
will provide in a supernatural way for the needs that are
impossible to meet in a natural way.

UNIQUE INDIVIDUALS

Let me share with you the personal satisfaction I have
received from a "quiver full" of children. Every one of my
four children is unique. The more children you have, the
more understanding you gain of the difference in personalities.

An honest effort has been made at our house not to
play favorites. I can honestly say that I love each of my
children with all of my heart. But I have learned that at
certain stages in each of their lives it has been harder to
get along with them. Since I tried to train each of them
alike, this was hard for me to understand.

One child learned early to make the bed without being
told. Others had to be reminded daily. One child hardly
ever got uptight over perfect grades, while other children
did. One child loved to read novels, while others loved to
read the newspaper. One was a natural when learning
directions and reading maps, while another got lost easily.
One child was outgoing, while another was very private.

I could go on and on. It has been fascinating to watch each child develop into a unique individual. The older they get the more I can see traits and talents like those found in my husband and me combined into our four children in so many different and unusual ways. What a blessing it is, though, that not one of them is a carbon copy of me. It is such a blessing to see the combination of us becoming "him" or "her." I'm learning to appreciate and to accept our differences.

CHILDREN ARE GOD'S GIFTS

Children are God's gifts intended to teach patience and compassion, forgiveness and humility. At times they are God's sandpaper, grating against my nerves and wishes. But again they have been like healing medicine that God has poured over my soul. My four children absorbed a lot of time over the years.

God used them to eliminate my selfishness. They constantly "demanded" that I tend to their needs. God used them to eliminate my laziness. Sometimes my very own children were rebellious.

God used them to eliminate my judgmental attitudes toward others. My children's varied talents and outlooks helped to eliminate my narrow outlook on life. Their mistakes and failures caused me to learn a deep faith in God.

They brought warmth and love and laughter at a time when I was concerned about making ends meet. They brought simplicity through lullabies and rocking horses at a time when I was weighed down with the problems of the world.

A "quiver full" of children brings many tears, but much laughter; less money, but more true worth; fewer new and shiny possessions, but much long-lasting joy; many hours of work, but more years of fulfillment.

Sharpen And Aim Your Arrows

Arrows are to shoot at the enemy. You have just a few brief years to sharpen your "arrows" and then to aim them at your enemy, the Devil. When your arrows leave your hand and your home there is nothing else you can do. It's so important that you sharpen them now. It's so important that you aim them straight before you let them fly. When you do let them go soaring through the air then you must trust God to guide them to their destination.

What I Desire As A Mother

Many years ago I wrote out in pencil on some scratch paper what I wanted to see in my children. I ran across it as I was writing this book. I still desire these things for my children. I think it would be a good idea for every mother to verbalize her deepest inner desires and to commit them to the Lord. I only share mine here in hope that it might inspire you to do the same.

1. I want my children to really "like" one another. I don't want this close relationship to end. I want the memories of childhood laughter and adventure to add spice to our family gatherings through the years.

2. I desire for the bond of Christian love to tie us all together. I want each of them to be devoted to the person of Jesus Christ and be filled with His Spirit. They don't have to grow up to be in my particular denomination, but I desire that we might not experience differences in doctrines that will divide our fellowship.

3. I desire that each of my children discover God's particular talents and spiritual gifts for them, and that they might be like garments that our Lord may readily put on to express Himself. May these talents never be channeled to the Devil's use or for self-glory. May each one first sacrifice the

"right to himself" to Jesus Christ. Then those gifts and talents will be "theirs and His forever."

4.   I want my children to learn to pray, win souls, minister to the needs of others, and see Jesus Christ on each page of the Bible.

5.   I "claim" for each of them a Christian husband or wife, filled with Your Spirit, for without You there can be no real unity.

CHAPTER FIVE

DURING THE PROCESS

The following segments are observations on raising my own children. I wrote these down shortly after they happened and record them here. Perhaps a look during the process will prove helpful.

LIFE AS IT IS

Today I don't have time to write, not even to sit down. Yet in the midst of all there is to do, I find great inspiration and must pause, even if it is at minute intervals, to put down these thoughts.

You see, if life wasn't so very ordinary and everyday, it might be amusing. I might wish the circumstances were different, or daydream them into nonexistence; but one fact would still be true – life is as it is – and nothing else.

I said I didn't have time to sit down – let me describe the circumstances that surround me at this very moment. My house is a complete wreck; my nineteen-month–old son, David, has caused many errors in my typing so far because of his reaching for me. He has a runny nose and is not feeling good. He just wants me to hold him. His five-year-old sister, Gayle, is talking incessantly, and it is hard for me even to concentrate.

I folded a "mountain" of clothes last night, while catching glimpses of a television program. The diapers are still on the couch. I was just too tired to put them up. The dishes from last night are staring at me too – plus the breakfast dishes. My daughter still lingers at my elbow with this pressing question, "When is Easter?" – which is still a month away. My boy is out of my lap, amused momentarily with a cookie.

Oh yes, I have a three-month-old baby, Janice, who (wonder of all wonders) is quiet at the moment, and a six-year-old son, Steve, who is in the first grade. Last night the nineteen-month-old woke up crying and would have no one but Ma Ma, and lo and behold, the baby woke up for her bottle also. Well, Daddy had to come to my assistance, for which I was deeply grateful. Then they both went back to sleep at the same time. This is really life as it is!

The rest of the house couldn't pass anyone's inspection, not even one room. Frankly, if someone came to see me right now, I would be downright ashamed to let them in. I do hope no one does, but wouldn't that really be just plain old "life"?

You might say to yourself, "My what a sloppy person," or "Life certainly couldn't be happy in that household." I beg to differ! (To be continued later – as the baby has stopped her amazing quietness. In fact, the nineteen-month-old is rocking the bassinette as he has seen me do.)

...I'm back – but it is six years later! You see, I really didn't have time to sit down that day. I put my original piece of paper I was typing in a drawer, and it has stayed there six years – along with other quickly scribbled items on various subjects.

I live in a different house now – even a different town. I have a laundry room with drawers to put my folded clothes in until I have time to put them up. I rarely go off if the dishes aren't washed. I also have a dishwasher, and the children are old enough to load it. The majority of the house is usually presentable in case company "happens" to drop in.

My "baby" started to school this year. It is awfully quiet around the house – at least until 2:00 p m. when school lets out. Life has slowed down somewhat for me, and I am beginning to find myself again. At times things are busy and at times frustrating, but they are very fulfilling.

TEAR-BRIMMED EYES

Only today did I comprehend how my own mother and father felt when I left home the first time to go to college. I'd never seen Daddy cry, but I still remember his eyes brimmed full with tears.

Today my oldest son left for school. Almost symbolic of his maturing and leaving the family nest, he literally lifted "wings" to fly. He not only left for school, but left by plane for England to be gone for eleven months.

I'm not prone to displays of emotion, but I knew as the days grew nearer that I would experience "something" when my number one son left home. Well, there were the tear-brimmed eyes that spilled over as we watched the steel-girded bird lift its wings and gradually disappear into the clouds.

As the family stood on the observation deck, we all bowed our heads as Dad lifted our hearts to heaven and committed him into the hands of his Heavenly Father. I prayed silently, "Oh God, teach him to do Your will."

How very thoughtful of our Father to paint a fantastic sunset as a grand send-off. Perhaps our son didn't see the sunset, for he was flying east; perhaps it was just for us who were left behind – a promise that Jesus would surely answer that prayer!

Second Child To College

I hadn't prepared myself when my second child left for school. Of course I had known she was leaving for months, and as the last few weeks and even few days drew near I was very calm and collected.

She was only going to be a little over an hour's drive away, so I hadn't thought a whole lot about missing her. I would still have two children at home, so I hadn't considered the "empty house" feeling.

When our oldest child left for school, he went across the ocean, and I knew there would be no weekend visits, no frequent phone calls. Because of this I had reckoned with that parting time weeks before it actually happened. I remember some of the emotional strings being cut as I prayed, giving him to the Lord's care.

The day we took Gayle to school was ideal. Everyone was calm and sweet and loving. We helped her move in and stayed until the finishing touches were put on the room. We went out for a lovely dinner – treating her to a T-bone steak. The day was then climaxed with prayers of dedication as we joined hands with her roommate and her roommate's parents.

It truly was the end to a perfect day, and we reminisced happily over the years as we drove back home. I wasn't prepared for the emotional letdown that followed on the next day. Perhaps I should have planned something special, but I just wanted to stay home. That's when it hit me that Gayle was gone – her room was so very *clean* and so very *empty*.

I knew I couldn't allow myself the indulgence of missing her already. No, I wouldn't call or write her. I just saw her yesterday. She would even be home for the weekend to go to a football game, so I would see her soon. I knew I shouldn't cry, so to compensate I decided to write my son, who lives quite a long way from home and can't get home for weekends.

Ironically, writing the letter just made me miss my son more than ever. I guess I transferred my emotions about my daughter over to him. The day finally ended, and we went to bed. I couldn't keep myself from thinking about Gayle. I didn't know why I was in the "weepy" mood. Later I realized that it was knowing deep within that a new relationship was beginning. Yes, I would see her often on weekends and vacations. But I knew it would never be the same again.

She and I had joked about the quote, "Some day you'll be a woman, dear." Was it that some of those motherly strings were being cut and I hadn't prepared myself for the "operation"? Anna Mow says that successful parenthood is working yourself out of a job. You're successful when your children don't need you any more.

I really *do* want to be a successful mother. I want my children to grow up – to be able to make wise decisions on their own. This involves steps toward freedom at the right time. Going to college is one of those right times to aid growing toward maturity. But who said that it wasn't normal to feel a little "pain" within when the strings of dependence are cut?

Most husbands handle their emotions in a different manner. I'm not a man, so I don't really know how they do it. But many women cry even when it is not an earth-shattering experience. It just seems to make us feel better. I just couldn't contain myself as we tried to go to sleep – so I slipped into the bathroom and closed the door and had a good cry. Then I prayed and committed her to the Lord. Everything seemed better, and I went back to bed and went to sleep.

Later.....Yes, the "operation" was a success. Adjustments were made. Gayle even came home several times.

Growing up has its hard times for both parent and child, but the rewards are tremendous. No one said that having children meant no problems, heartache, or even sorrow. But God promised that if we'd bring them up in the fear and admonition of the Lord it would be very rewarding. Children are one of God's unique plans for bringing happiness to our lives.

THE TAMING OF THE WILD OX

The analogy of the "wild ox" is hidden away in a description of the omnipotence of God (Job 39:9-12). The first time I studied this Scripture my oldest son was overseas at school, preparing to come home. He was at a time in his life of asserting his independence and becoming his own man. Job asks the question:

> Will the unicorn (wild ox) be willing to serve thee, or abide by thy crib? Canst thou bind the unicorn (wild ox) with his band in the furrow? Or will he harrow the valleys after thee? Wilt thou trust him, because his strength is great? Or wilt thou leave thy labour to him? Wilt thou believe him, that he will bring home thy seed, and gather it into thy barn?

God spoke to my heart that day with this analogy, saying:

> Your son is your "wild ox" –
>   wanting to be free
>   to make his own decisions.
>
> And the answer is no! The
>   "wild ox" won't be willing
>   to serve you, to abide by
>   your crib.
> No! You can't bind your
>   "wild ox" to you.
> No! You can't trust him to
>   bring home your seed into
>   your barn –

> even though his
> strength is great.
>
> No! The "wild ox" can't and
> won't! But the *tame* ox will.
>
> And I'm the only One who can
> tame him. I've been *using* you
> all these years, but today
> I want to make it very clear,
> you must trust Me implicitly
> to complete the job of the
> "taming of the wild ox."
> If you do - I promise you that
> I'll do it.

With full assurance I committed the job to God's hands. If there was ever a time that I believed God for anything it was that day. It's exciting every time I think about it. The Lord has been doing a marvelous job.

Our son came home from school with a desire to help in our ministry. For four months we experienced the fulfillment of the promise God gave to me, as our son made a valuable contribution to our work by eagerly helping in the youth ministry of the church. It was so good to have him home again with a prospect of being with us two more years.

At the end of four months the Lord called us to another state. Since Steve didn't wish to come we left him behind in college. The Lord knew what He was doing, for our "wild ox" began to mature and to serve Him in a youth ministry uniquely suited to his talents and personality.

I never quite felt that those four months were all God had in mind – and like Mary, I pondered in my heart this Scripture from time to time. Down deep I knew there was more to come if I kept believing and waiting on God. Later the Lord showed me another Scripture to link with the one in Job. It was a further encouragement when I had times of doubt. Proverbs 14:4 says, "Where no oxen are, the crib is clean; but much increase is by the strength of the ox." Yes, there would be problems of all sizes and kinds, ranging from clothes on the floor to whether or not he should marry before finishing college.

Well, he *did* marry (that's another story) and moved near us for a couple of years. He visisted frequently after that – but on a new basis. His judgments were wiser and his lifestyle maturing. I prayed that he'd love our new home, and the church, and friends, and that our family would continue to enjoy one another.

There was an inward rejoicing during those days, as I saw God faithfully fulfilling His promise. I saw evidence of the "taming of the wild ox." Yes, my son is no longer a boy; he is a man. And I like what I see! I "clipped strings" a little at a time for years. Some were more painful than others, but there was a release and an inward peace, knowing the operation would be successful. Oh, it doesn't mean that we are alike in every area. But it means that I have great confidence in what God is doing in Steve's unique life.

One day many years ago, God pointed His finger at the following Scripture: "The father of the righteous shall greatly rejoice: and he that begetteth a wise child shall have joy of him. Thy father and thy mother shall be glad, and she that bare thee shall rejoice" (Proverbs 23:24-25). With overflowing joy I made this entry by this passage – "Thank you, Lord!"

"Where no oxen are the crib is clean," but what good is a clean crib without oxen? Why do you want oxen in the first place, when they cause a great deal of mess and trouble? Well, "much increase is by the strength of the ox." When the "wild ox" is *tamed* he brings *much* increase.

I can't describe the fulfillment that comes from experiencing the taming of a "wild ox" – from seeing what God can do, then witnessing the increase that God brings – the love for family and for Jesus, a life given over to serving Him. I know I've just begun my rejoicing, for God gave assurance for all in that verse in Proverbs 14:4, "Much increase is by the strength of the ox." And to think that God allowed me to be a vital part of His taming process. What a privilege! But I must remember all the time that He said, "Without me you can do nothing" (John 15:5).

PRACTICAL POINTERS FOR OX TAMING

Listed below are hints that I've found valuable in the taming of four "wild oxen." Yes, I have made many mistakes, but with prayer, confession of these mistakes, and many brand new beginnings, it has been an exciting adventure.

1. Receive your "basic" instruction from God's Word. There is no substitute for a daily searching of the Bible and discovering specific precepts and promises for your child (Deuteronomy 6:6-9).

2. After the study of God's Word, gain insights in training children from Christian books. Be sure to check all the principles in these books by the Word of God (Proverbs 11:14).

3. Discipline with fairness and consistency. Provide guidelines based on God's Word. Have mercy for genuine repentance. Use physical correction only when other methods won't work. Maintain a "positive" atmosphere in your home. Don't discipline in anger (Proverbs 23:13, TLB; Proverbs 29:25; Ephesians 6:4).

4. Lead your child to Jesus at an early age and encourage him in Christian growth and involvement in Christian activities and service for the Lord (2 Timothy 3:15; Proverbs 23:15-16).

5. Understand and appreciate the individuality of your child. Help him have a healthy evaluation of his temperament, talents, spiritual gifts, role, and phase of life.

6. Recognize the importance of training your child in the ability to make decisions. Release him a little at a time so when he is college age he will be ready to handle important decisions (Proverbs 22:6).

7. Be available to share in your child's problems and joys – his defeats and achievements. Be genuinely interested and always have a "listening ear."

8. Teach by example how to confess wrongs and to ask for and to give forgiveness as the way to bring unity between family, friends, and foes (Ephesians 4:32).

9. Teach your child to establish priorities and time scheduling. Help him to be well-rounded in his outlook on life, not neglecting or "blowing out of proportion" any area (Proverbs 23:22-23; Ecclesiastes 12:1).

10. Teach responsibility and basic skills helpful to the future role. Chores that are appropriate to the age of the child teach the importance of work. Learning basic skills such as washing dishes, cleaning bathrooms and windows, mowing the lawn or sweeping the patio will aid in being responsible for "all" of one's workload later and eliminate frustration due to ignorance of simple how to's (Proverbs 10:5).

11. Provide an atmosphere of praise and joy in your home. Teach your child to praise the Lord at all times. This is best taught by example – you should practice it in word and song. Be a "tra la la la la" family (Psalm 34:1,3; 90:14).

12. Pursue any avenue of interest and provide training to develop talents of your child. Use books, hobbies, travel, music lessons, swimming or tennis lessons to help discover these areas. Undeveloped talents will create frustrations in later life. Encourage him by rejoicing in accomplishments.

13. Teach by attitude, example, and definite instruction an appreciation and respect for the opposite sex. Appropriate books for various ages are available to help you bridge communication gaps, but aren't a substitute for heart-to-heart talks (Proverbs 23:26-27; 5:18-21).

14. Help your child discover God's will for his life. Show him that true fulfillment comes in doing God's will instead of through fame, prosperity, pleasure, or beauty (Ecclesiastes 12:1).

15. Teach the value of "hiding God's Word" in your heart. Show the importance of Bible study, Scripture memory, and most of all how to make real and practical the Scriptures for daily living (Psalm 119:9,11).

16. Guide your child in the importance of godly friends (Proverbs 1:10, 15; 22:24-25; 23:19-21).

17. Set an example of love by loving your husband (Titus 2:4).

18. Spend time having fun together – games, watching sports, picnics, trips. Have a sense of humor. Let laughter ring through your home daily (Job 8:21; Psalm 126:2).

19. Provide encouragement. Be a motivator. Rejoice in your child's accomplishments and growth in all areas – physical, psychological, and spiritual (Proverbs 23:15-16, 24-25).

Plants Grown Up

May our sons be like plants
    grown up in their youth;
Their foliage the rich leaves
    of pureness and truth.

Branches grown full
    to give needed shade
For those whose lives
    with burdens are weighed.

Lord, they must be rooted
    and grounded in Thee;

If they would grow up
    in *Thy* likeness to be.

May they be watered from
    Your fountain of truth;
So our plants won't be dwarfed
    They'll grow up in their youth.

That our sons may be like plants grown up in their youth.
Psalm 144:12

Polished Cornerstones

God gave me two special daughters
    Like stones, yet unshaped and unhewn;
Hidden were charm and beauty inside
    With patience, I'd see some day soon.

One must have a delicate touch
    For polishing stones so fine;
Yes, God has a place of honor
    For these lovely daughters of mine.

May our daughters be like cornerstones
    When the polishing process is through;
Sparkling, radiant, and ready for use
    In the King's very palace it's true.

That our daughters may be as cornerstones,
polished after the similitude of a palace
Psalm 144:12

BEAUTIFUL CONFIRMATION

I had arrived for a three-day stay with my son's future in-laws. A wedding was scheduled in four months, and Tennessee and Florida were pretty far apart for much planning together. While I was there the future bride and groom were to arrive for a day off from nearby colleges.

The mother and father of the bride were previous acquaintances and fellow church members. It was such a joy to be in their home and to experience the fellowship we had those few days. The mother-in-law, June, graciously shared the plans that were being made and asked for any suggestions. I didn't intend to make a nuisance of myself, so I had not planned any suggestions before I came.

Nevertheless I was delighted when she invited me to compose the words for the wedding invitation. We thought it would be nice if we based it on a Scripture verse that meant something special. As June and I were sharing one afternoon, a verse came to her that God had shown her several years before and given to her as a promise for her son and daughter:

> That our sons may be like plants grown up in their youth; that our daughters may be like cornerstones polished after the similitude of a palace. (Psalm 144:12)

I was so excited, because I had written two poems about that verse several years before. I had written a date in my Bible claiming it as a promise for *my* sons and daughters. Another exciting thing about this verse is that neither one of us had ever heard a sermon or read an article on it. We had both discovered it in our personal devotions.

When my future daughter-in-law Cindi, and Steve got home we were sharing about "our" verse. They both concluded we should use this verse on the invitation. It was a beautiful confirmation. The next morning was Sunday. When I woke up, the verse, "Every good gift and every perfect gift is from above" (James 1:17) was on my heart. On the way to church I remarked, "Let me share my verse for today." And when I did – what do you think happened? June had that verse underlined in *her* Bible too. We rejoiced together that God had made us of one mind and heart. We decided to use that verse at the top of the invitation and Psalm 144:12 at the bottom.

I suppose the climax to the weekend came when we all gathered around the dining table for prayer before we went to bed. It was such a sweet time as our children thanked the Lord for their parents. Then we all asked God to bless their wedding. I believe I knew that night God was going to do something special in their wedding. I was eager to watch it unfold in the days to come.

HIS PRESENCE IS REQUESTED

Two young people grown up, in love, and committed to Jesus Christ! What kind of wedding was it to be? Yes, Cindi and Steve wanted Jesus to be glorified, to be a very real part of their wedding. From the beginning of the plans the invitation had been issued – "*His* presence is requested."

They wanted a wedding that would uniquely express their personalities and tastes and still magnify *Him*. Of course they wanted a beautiful wedding, but nothing pretentious. They wanted a message to be communicated to all who came. That message was that their home was to be founded and built upon Jesus Christ, the Living Word of God and the Bible, His written Word.

The open Bible was selected as the most fitting symbol to express the message of their wedding. A tremendous blessing was gained as this symbol began to permeate the preparation. The open Bible became the literal as well as the spiritual focal point of the wedding ceremony.

A TIME OF WORSHIP

Some of the unique parts of the ceremony were as follows: A young man who was a close friend was the emcee. He led *A Time of Worship*. He welcomed everyone on behalf of Cindi and Steve and in the name of Jesus. He then led the congregation in a Scripture song of praise (Psalm 103:1)

After the processional the bride was seated on the front left side between her parents; the groom was seated on the front right between his parents. The attendants were seated in a semicircle on the platform, facing the audience.

A TIME OF THANKSGIVING AND BLESSING

Next was an especially meaningful *Time of Thanksgiving and Blessing*. The groom introduced those who were in the wedding party. He then expressed words of appreciation to all those who had been a blessing in his and Cindi's lives.

A song was sung to set the stage for words of "blessing" spoken by friends and relatives. These people gave a one-minute blessing in the name of the Lord for the bride and groom. Two of these blessings follow:

> The world knows a lot about the word happiness, but little do they know about the word joy. This is the blessing I have for you: That your lives should manifest joy, not just happiness and good times, but celestial, hilarious joy together as you experience the resurrected Christ and His power in your lives – George Baldwin

> God knows every need before it arises. His provisions are not only sure, but they're full and overflowing, so that you may confess with the psalmist, "I shall not want." I know that both of you will see with a vision denied to many because your hearts are pure and the promise is given to the pure in heart that "they shall see God." – Louie Hall

A TIME OF COMMITMENT

The final part of the service was a *Time of Commitment*. The emcee came and stood in the middle of the church. The parents and the bride and groom stood. The emcee said, "The Bible says, 'A man shall leave his father and his mother and shall cleave to his wife.' " The groom stepped forward at this point, symbolizing this Scripture. The emcee then said "The Bible also says, 'He that giveth her in marriage doeth well.' " The bride, accompanied by her father, stepped forward to join the groom. After declaring his intentions by giving his daughter to be married, the father of the bride then asked the audience to join him in prayer as he thanked God for the couple and presented them to God to be married.

The bride and groom joined the minister on the platform. A declaration of intention was given by the bride and groom. The wedding vows were then given by the bride and groom to each other.

Groom: The Scripture says in Ephesians 5:25-29, "Husbands, love your wives, even as Christ also loved the church, and gave Himself for it; that He might sanctify and cleanse it with the washing of water by the word. That He might present it to Himself a glorious church, not having spot, or wrinkle, or any such thing; but that it should be holy and without blemish. So ought men to love their wives as their own bodies. He that loveth his wife loveth himself."

Cindi, on the basis of this Scripture and with the aid of the Holy Spirit, I commit myself to love you as Christ loved the church, sacrificially and totally; to set you apart from and above all others; to be your example and to encourage you in all things; to be concerned about your own special needs as I am about those of my own body. Therefore I commit myself to you and I receive you as my wife, completor, and my friend. I receive you as God's gracious gift to me from our Lord Jesus Christ.

Bride: The Bible says in Ephesians 5:22-24, "Wives, submit yourselves unto your own husbands, as unto the Lord. For the husband is the head of the wife, even as Christ is the head of the church; and He is the Savior of the body. Therefore as the church is subject unto Christ, so let the wives be to their own husbands in everything."

Steve, on the basis of God's Word and with the aid of the Holy Spirit, I commit myself to you to be a completor and helpmeet. I promise to submit myself in joyful obedience to you, even as the church is subject to Christ. With His help I will minister to your needs in times of adversity as well as times of joy. Nothing will take me from your side except death itself. Today, Steve, I receive and accept you as God's gracious gift to me.

The Scripture portion of the vows was read from the big, open Bible which was on a stand between the minister and the bride and groom. After the vows the bride and groom exchanged rings and repeated the ring vows. The minister then gave words of admonition and spiritual good wishes for the bride and groom. He used these words that I had written for them:

Our Wishes For You

We wish for you *love* – deep and abiding, but light-hearted and overflowing.

We wish for you *joy* – that bubbles in the fun times, but remains to sustain through pain and sorrow.

We wish for you *true companionship* – that can communicate for hours or simply sit and be contented in the silence of each other's presence.

We wish for you a *oneness* – not that will destroy each unique person, but when joined together will make a winning team.

We wish for you a *superior lifestyle* – cherishing your heritage, appreciating and drawing from the very best qualities of your families, until you form one united for your needs, better far together than you would have possessed alone.

We wish for you *faith* – in one another, so deep that any whispered, ungrounded rumor cannot penetrate its foundation. But most of all a faith in God – so grounded and rooted in a love for Jesus Christ that your love for one another will seem small in its presence – but in reality will be greater than it ever could have been because of His great resources to draw upon.

We wish for you *to know and do God's will for your lives* – not living selfishly to only satisfy your needs, but to discover how you may "reach out" together to this world in need.

We wish for you the *joy of children* – like the joy that we have known, not expecting that life will be easier because of them but richer and wiser and more satisfying; for God has given them to us not only to teach but to be our teachers – to reflect not only our strengths but to glaringly show us our weaknesses.

We wish for you such *inner charm and beauty* – that each wrinkle and gray hair will not detract from your relationship but only make the other dearer in your sight.
And if there be *greater joys and hopes and goals* that we have not fathomed as yet – we wish them all for you –

> Our cherished son, Steve
> and now cherished
> "daughter-in-law," Cindi.

We bless you with the greatest of human love that we know – in the name of our Lord Jesus Christ!

The groom was then invited to pray and ask God's blessings upon his new home. His prayer was as follows:

Lord God, I ask you to bless our home and our marriage. Give us love one for the other. Let that love stem from You. Lord, as we place our hands upon this Bible, symbolizing the rock of Your Word, our lives being built on the firm foundation of Your

Word, I pray that you will give us the strength to live up to each commitment and vow we have made. I just thank You for the love You have given us for each other. In Jesus' name I pray, Amen!

This wedding didn't just happen. Much prayer was offered and much planning took place. The wishes of the bride and groom were foremost in the planning. Both families were also consulted and included. It was fun!

It was exciting to me to see how Christian young people could become involved in planning a Christ-honoring wedding while at the same time expressing their individual tastes and talents.

Of course it was a special time for me as mother and mother-in-law to be welcomed with love into this planning. I suppose I received as great a spiritual blessing as anyone throughout the joyous occasion.

This is just one example of how a wedding can be unique *and* Christ-honoring. Who is the first person you will invite to your wedding, or to your son's or daughter's wedding? Don't forget:

His presence is requested!

(Ideas were gleaned from other weddings that had been a special blessing. *Special thanks* to the following: *Debbie and Richard Lord* and their families – for the ideas of the bride and groom seated between their parents and stepping forward, symbolizing "leaving father and mother" and the words of thanksgiving and blessing. *Lynn and Cary Bates* – for a portion of their original wedding vows.)

INGREDIENTS FOR A CHRIST-HONORING WEDDING

The following are some ingredients for a Christ-honoring wedding. If some of these are missing, Christ can still be honored, but the more of them that are present, the greater the blessing will be.

1. Two committed Christian young people who are deeply in love. (Not optional.)

2. Two committed Christian families excited about the uniting of these two lives.

3. A desire on the part of each of the former to have a Christ-honoring wedding.

4. A communication established between all parties involved.

5. A symbol chosen to communicate the main message of the wedding.

6. An involvement of as many members of the family as possible.

7. Involvement of Christian friends who would add a spiritual dimension to the wedding.

A BOND OF LOVE ACROSS THE MILES

My son David has always been the typical calm, cool, and collected type. But in his younger years, he did not show much excitement about any activity. One of the prayers I prayed for him all year was that the Lord would motivate him into action.

It seemed like he retreated into his room and played his guitar in most of his spare moments. Of course, I didn't know exactly what he did behind his closed doors.

As the year progressed, he expressed an interest in going overseas for the summer with a missions organization called "Operation Mobilization." We began to pray that God would lead him in this decision. He and another friend continued to talk and pray about the summer. David felt a confirmation that this was God's will. Quite a large amount of money had to be raised. But he couldn't directly ask for financial support, but only for prayer support. It was also specified that he or his family couldn't give over a certain amount. The rest had to come in answer to prayer.

He emptied his savings; we gave what we could and he prayed and waited.

The time drew very near, and all his money wasn't in. But little by little it came – five dollars or ten, then fifty and more. At last the day came when all his support was given. How we praised God for answered prayer!

He discovered that those who played the guitar could take it along. Some of them might get to be in musical groups. I was beginning to see the reason David had been playing his guitar so much. Later as he chose the country to which he was to go, it really made sense. He was able to join a musical group going to Austria for the summer. Part of their witnessing opportunities developed by going door to door singing and playing.

Finally the day arrived on which David was to leave. I had asked each member of the family to find Bible verses to be claimed on David's behalf and bring them to break-fast that morning. They were then given as words of blessing in Jesus' name. As each one shared his blessing, there was a bond of love created to stretch across the miles. Then David got his guitar and sang for us a little song he had written that morning. Needless to say there were tears in all our eyes:

> Now the time has come
>   when I must finally say goodbye;
> You know it breaks my heart
>   to see the sadness in your eyes;
> But soon the time will come
>   when even time will be no more
> And all of us will join to sing
>   our praises to the Lord.
> You know I hate to go, but again I
>   feel the call
> To go and tell the world about
>   the Savior of us all,

> The harvest is so ripe
> and the workers are so few;
> And I guess to tell them
> is the least that I can do.
> So please remember me when you
> kneel down to pray,
> Remember I will think of you
> through each and every day;
> And now that I've said all of this
> I've only one thing more –
> I love you more than anything
> in all this great big world.
> – David Rogers

Then he left, and each day we prayed and waited for a letter. How thrilled we were when we heard how God was using David. He asked us to pray for Rupert, Helfried, and Berti. He told us how they went door to door singing, playing and sharing the gospel; how they had Bible studies for the local young people.

His nineteenth birthday came while he was overseas. I packed a box full of surprises and prayed that God would communicate our love across the miles.

After two months the day came for him to come back home. Of course we were all excited. We talked for hours that first night. It was a long time before he "ran down." Truly God had motivated David. A vision for reaching people for Christ around the world had been planted in his heart, and he will never be the same. He came back home with a desire to go and tell about Jesus right here in Memphis, Tennessee.

He still prays for some of his Austrian friends to grow in their knowledge of Christ, though now he is a missionary in Spain with his wife and children.

THE SOUND OF MUSIC

He hath put a new song in my mouth, even praise unto our God: many shall see it, and fear, and shall trust in the LORD. (Psalm 40:3)

Ever since I can remember I have loved to sing. I never thought I had any great talent for singing, but it was always a part of my life. Sometimes it was a hymn sung in church, or other times just humming a tune while I worked. I, nevertheless, agreed with the songwriter who wrote, "Without a song the day would never end."

It was no wonder when I had my children that the "sound of music" was heard throughout our home. I sang to them when I rocked them as babies. As they grew older we sang together as we took walks. I even got them a little record player so they could play records for themselves. I still remember lots of the little songs we sang.

My husband bought me a used piano so I could learn how to play. I was teaching myself, but it was too hard to learn much that way, so I started taking lessons. However, I already had one child; then came number two, then three, four, and finally five. There wasn't much time for piano lessons in those days, so I dropped them. But we still had the piano that I played a little from time to time. Because it was there, the children began music lessons one by one.

Then our home literally rang with the "sound of music." All of the children took piano for as long as they were interested. Then the two boys also took up guitar and later began composing music.

Our youngest daughter, Janice, loved to sit at the piano and play and sing. And I loved to hear this lovely "sound of music." Janice was a teenager when she first saw the movie, "The Sound of Music." She really liked the

movie and, of course, the music. She got a songbook and
also a record of "The Sound of Music." She played all the
songs on the piano and sang and sang until she had
memorized them all. She almost wore out her record. The
song she loved the most was "My Favorite Things."

Janice also loved to play the piano and sing songs
about the Lord. She trusted Jesus when she was just a
little girl and liked to praise the Lord through her music.
There were times of tears and heartache – like the time
she had to move away from her favorite friend, Jill, and
the time when her favorite dog, Tawny, died. She combined the melody to this favorite song with her love for
Jesus and wrote these beautiful words:

> Joy thru my teardrops, and gains thru my losses
> Beauty for ashes, and crowns for my crosses.
> He binds my wounds, and He dries all my tears
> Calms every storm and He conquers my fears.
>
> He gives me hinds' feet to walk on high places.
> He floods my soul with His heavenly graces.
> When I am weak then His strength makes me strong.
> I know I can trust Him, He's never been wrong.
>
> Trials may come and temptations assail me;
> Though I may falter, He never will fail me.
> So Satan I bind you in His holy name
> For at the cross Jesus' blood overcame!
>
> When the doubt comes, when I'm lonely,
> When my heart is sad.
> I'll lift up mine eyes to my Saviour above
> And Jesus will make me glad.
>
> *Verse Two*
> When in my heart there is sadness and sorrow
> Jesus has promised a brighter tomorrow.
> Victory is mine, Yes, it's already won.
> I've only to claim it by faith in God's Son.

All of my cares I will cast down before Him
Even in trials my heart will adore Him.
He bears my burdens, He comforts my soul
Oh why should I worry when He's in control?

Lord in the time of deep grief and emotion
I will yet serve You with constant devotion.
You have not failed me one step of the way;
That is the reason I'll trust You and say:

I will praise You! I will praise You!
Jesus Christ my King;
For You fill my heart with a song in the night;
Yes, You make my heart to sing![1]

– Janice Rogers Edmiston

Truly our lives have been greatly blessed through the "sound of music."

"LORD, IT WOULD BE REAL NICE!"

Delight thyself also in the Lord; and He shall give thee the desires of thine heart. (Psalm 37:4)

I had arrived! It was just the second day of the New Year, and I had already become a grandmother. I had heard from *lots* of people that "grandmothering" is the ultimate in all of this life's experiences.

God certainly gave me "the desires of my heart" with the gift of being a grandparent.

My husband and I had ten days vacation time to wait for our first grandchild. So we boarded the airplane the day after Christmas and headed for Florida. I didn't want to pray selfishly, but I *did* tell the Lord my desires. I said that it surely would be nice if the baby could be born while we were there. After we arrived we visited and waited; and waited and visited. We then decided to take a little trip and visit friends. I didn't want to go very far. Since I had come all the way from Tennessee to Florida, I wanted to be at the hospital when the baby came.

The weekend came and went and still no baby. We all thought maybe Cindi would have the first baby of the New Year. But New Year's Day came and went and still no baby. We also wanted to visit *our* parents who lived three hours away. I hated to leave with the baby due so soon, but we had planned to go the next morning.

But at 4:15 a.m. the next morning, a knock came at our bedroom door. Steve said, "We're getting ready to go to the hospital." The first words that came to my mind were, "a time to be born" (Ecclesiastes 3:2). We got up and my husband led in prayer as we all held hands. Then Steve took Cindi to the hospital. I wanted to go too, but this was Steve and Cindi's hour together. We would go to the hospital later. As we went back to bed, I said, "It seems like we should do *something*." My husband jokingly said, "Well, boil some water then." I finally got to sleep after reminiscing about when I had *my* first child.

We were all staying with Cindi's parents so after breakfast we all went to the hospital and waited in the waiting room. The following was what took place while we were there:

A Time to Be Born

"She's doing fine –
   Yes, he's fine too."

Sitting and waiting!

"It's not quite time.
   Just be patient."

Reading and praying

"Yes, Doctor, nice to meet you,
   Good, it won't be long."

Waiting and watching!
"It's a girl!
        Blue eyes, lots of hair."
Thanking and praising!

Cindi had the baby by natural childbirth, so Steve was able to be with her all the time. Then after the baby was born he could stay with them for about an hour. The grandparents were allowed to go in to see the baby and the parents for five minutes. She was so beautiful. Of course I would think so. I'm her grandmother! We went to the nursery later and looked and looked and took lots of pictures.

Thank you Lord, for giving me the desires of my heart - to be able to be there when "our" baby was born and to visit with Cindi and Steve and our grandparents-in-law. It was all so very special!

Now my husband and I are the proud grandparents of eight grandchildren. It's just my husband and I now in our home. The children long gone with their families to raise. I remember the day, when I prayed, "Lord, it would be real nice!" Indeed, my quiver is full!

NOTE

1.   © Copyright 1980 – Janice Rogers. All rights reserved.

CHAPTER SIX

THE LORD SHALL CHOOSE FOR ME

He shall choose our inheritance for us...
Psalm 47:4

Not what I wish to be
Nor where I wish to go
For who am I
That I should choose my way?
The Lord shall choose for me
Tis better far I know
Then let Him bid me go or stay.[1]

As a teenager I felt God leading me into a full-time Christian vocation. It later developed that the particular field was to be a minister's wife. I loved all phases of church work, so I knew I would be happy.

Adrian and I were married while still in college and he was called to a small country church. We were happy there, serving the Lord as we continued our schooling. I taught all the teenagers and helped conduct a Christian recreation program on Saturday evenings.

After three years we moved to the seminary. While there we were called to another small church. I continued to teach all the teenagers, sing, and visit with my husband.

With schooling behind and three additions to our family, we were called to a somewhat larger church – our first full-time pastorate. Life became involved as different jobs in the church opened and my family grew even larger. But I was very happy even though these years were busy ones – raising a family and serving the Lord. Our church grew, but was still an average-size church. I felt at home there.

We were then called to a church with fewer in attendance but with a great potential for growth. We knew God had called us there! The Lord began to bless. He added more and more to His church in that place.

I began to feel a little apprehension. It was an evasive feeling. I had never wanted to go to a big church. I had voiced that feeling several times. Outwardly I was able to keep up appearances. The Lord has since shown me that I was inwardly fearful – fearful of being unneeded, of being outgrown, of not being capable, fearful of being shut out of my husband's time. The more the church grew, the more he was gone.

One day I discovered that this wasn't the role I had chosen so willingly. This wasn't the role I loved and was so comfortable in. Self-pity crept into my life - even resentment. I became frustrated. Many feelings I had seldom experienced bombarded me. At times I would feel a deep loneliness, even when surrounded by hundreds of people. I longed for someone to understand. Pride kept me from admitting to anyone else and even myself that I was dissatisfied with my role.

I couldn't admit it then, but it is as if I said to God, "I didn't choose this plan. I want another version altered to my specifications. I don't believe You can re-adjust and enlarge my life to fit into Your plan."

So God grabbed the rug and snatched it from under me. It was as if He replied, "You thought you could do something – but not this. You can't do anything without Me."

He taught me some wonderful truths in those days spent "lying on the floor." I felt so defeated. The Lord never deals with us alike. That is why we shouldn't be too enamored with someone else's experience. You see, He knows exactly which corner of the "rug" to pull, and just how hard we can fall without permanent damage. That's why we can't open our own little "Rug-Pulling Company," thinking we will play God in the lives of our friends. We always seem to snatch the wrong corner of the "rug."

God is totally sufficient to deal with your family and friends Himself. So you had better let your "Rug-Pulling Company" go bankrupt and just offer your services to God to be a helper in the pick-up business. I didn't realize then what God was doing. In fact, I had recovered much faster from other experiences with God's "Rug-Pulling Company."

When God snatched the "rug" through the death of my third baby, I had instantly looked up and seen Him standing there with His hand outstretched saying "Get up my child, and lean hard on Me." And I did! Immediately I recognized that there was nothing I could do.

Yes, God was using His sure-win method on me. He was bringing me to the end of myself. You can come the long way or take the short cut – whichever way you choose. But if you are a child of God, you will eventually come to the end of yourself and arrive at the way out of your problem.

The way out is Jesus Christ! If only I had believed, He could have made me adequate in the first place. Now I have discovered the long, hard way that He is able. "I can do all things through Christ which strengtheneth me" (Philippians 4:13).

I had memorized those words as a teenager. If anyone knew their meaning, I thought I did! But did I really? Sometimes we profit through taking the long way to the end of ourselves. Then we are more inclined to stay off the long way in the future. We are more willing to say, "Lord, send me to the entrance of the path where I got off the shortcut. I want to stand there and guard the entrance and tell others, 'Don't enter here. I've been this way before and it only leads to disappointment. Here, let me point you to the shortcut.' "

Don't ever run to find as many people as you can to whom you can tell your experience. You will have to leave your post to do that. God has stationed you there. He will show you when and where to warn.

Some people are just looking for a dramatic experience that they can tell. I heard a lady tell someone, "I always wanted a testimony I could share in public – now I have one." Every time I passed her, sure enough, she was telling someone new about her experience. And she was filling in details that should have been buried at the feet of Jesus.

Praise God for our experience with Jesus Christ. But those experiences were intended to help bring you to the end of yourself and to point you to the way out. Jesus Himself. They were intended to make you a gatekeeper to point others to the shortcut, who is Jesus. If you find yourself looking at your experience more than at the way out, something is wrong.

When we finally come to the way out, what then? Have you learned anything along the path? I finally said when I got to Jesus Christ and stopped trying my own shortcuts, "Lord, I'm totally dependent on You. I didn't choose this way, but You know best. I'm going to believe that You can enlarge my life – make me supernaturally adequate. I'm going to stop saying 'I can't' and say 'You can.' "

I know that it works. It was 1970 that I stood at the end of myself and looked into the face of Jesus with nowhere else to go. It is miraculous what He has done in and through my life in areas in which I was so inadequate.

In fact, about a year after I allowed the Lord to control my defeated life, a "call" came to go to a really large church. It was one like I had always secretly dreaded. My first reaction was, "Oh no!" I remember saying those words out loud. Then I could almost feel God's hand on my shoulder as He whispered, "Don't be a fool, after all I have shown you in the past year."

That was enough reminder for me. Even before my husband knew for sure, down deep I knew that God wanted us to go. The greatest of all miracles was that I was willing to go or stay. The Lord gave me a great inner peace that everything was going to be all right. That doesn't mean that there was no hurt involved in the move. It has always been hard to move. The only way I can describe it is that it is like an operation. Part of my life was amputated. It was painful.

We lived on an island, and we had to cross a bridge to leave our home of eight years. Things had gone pretty well all morning. I had kept busy with packing and cleaning, but when we crossed the bridge, I could almost feel the knife cutting away that part of my life. I couldn't stop the tears that flowed. "It's all right, Lord, I know You want us to go but I'm leaving a part of me back there." The lovely memories will always be with me, but a brand new chapter in my life was beginning.

No one said much for several miles. What we all felt inside was too private to talk about at that moment. But after a while the stabbing pain of separation was over. The operation was a success. God gave a sweet assurance of His presence.

It's an odd feeling, being "in-between." I didn't know except by faith whether others at the end of the destination would love me like those I had just left. I wondered how the children would adapt. The youngest two, David and Janice, moved with us. The two teenagers, Gayle and Steve, were left behind, one for just two months and the other to go to college.

Their lives were radically changed because of our sudden move. This all caused doubts. However I had an

inward peace about God's leading. I would commit each
difficulty to the Lord as it arose. Only He really knew what
lay ahead.

> Submission to the will
> Of Him who guides me still
> Is surety of His love revealed.
> My soul shall rise above
> This world in which I move;
> I conquer only where I yield.[2]

LOOKING BACK

I could never have told you that day how God would
honor that commitment made by faith. The love that waited
for me in this huge church was more than I could fathom.
Since my marriage I have never lived very near my mother,
but Memphis, Tennessee, was a thousand miles away from
home. But there were many "mothers" who patted me and
told me that they loved me. I felt like asking them, "How do
you know you love me? You don't even know me yet."

But they did love me! They loved me by faith, and they
continue to love me. Indeed, it was amazing how everyone
moved in to fill the void created by my recent "operation."
Yes, I responded to that love. Soon that "loving by faith"
became a reality.

NOTES

1.   C. Austin Miles, "Submission" (The Rodeheaver Co., copyright
     renewal 1962). Used by permission.
2.   Ibid.

CHAPTER SEVEN

A WISE WOMAN
BUILDS BRIDGES

BUILDING BRIDGES THROUGH PRAYER

A wise woman builds bridges to others in her community, her nation, and in her world. The chief means by which all ministry is accomplished is through prayer. This is our avenue of communication with the dependence on our Lord. It isn't the position of our bodies, but the attitude of our hearts that really matters.

We must come to Him first with *meekness*. Jesus said, "Blessed are the meek; for they shall inherit the earth" (Matthew 5:5). This means our spirits will be submissive, easily guided and controlled by the Lord. The blessings of meekness run through the whole Bible.

The Blessings of Submission

Blessed are they who demonstrate
    a submissive spirit (Ephesians 5:21-24).
Blessed are they who do not seek
    to assert their own rights (Matthew 16:24-25).
Blessed are they who recognize
    their God-given position
    and do not covet
    another's place (1 Corinthians 11:3).

Blessed are they who do not
    accuse God of giving
    them an inferior
    position (Genesis 2:18; 3:16).
Blessed are they who, like Christ
    react with love to those
    who *do* abuse their authority
    and look with scorn at others (Matthew 5:10-12)
Blessed are they who, under Christ,
    work to correct abuses
    to others, but do not
    attempt to change
    God-given roles (Matthew 5:43-46).
Blessed are they who are under
    authority; for they shall
    be over (Matthew 8:8-10).
Blessed are they who find their
    true identity, self-worth
    and equality in Jesus Christ
    and not by proving their
    abilities (Galatians 3:28).
Blessed are they who do not seek
    to "save their own lives,"
    but look to God to promote
    their cause (Psalm 75:6-7).
Blessed are they who do not seek
    to explain away the principles
    of God's Word to suit one's
    own cause (Titus 2:4-5).
Blessed are they who have confidence
    in the example of Christ
    as being equal with God the
    Father – not inferior, though
    submissive to Him (1 Corinthians 15:24-28;
    Philippians 2:5-11).
Blessed are they who are willing
    to be controlled by a higher
    authority –

for they of all
   people on this earth
    shall find fulfillment (Matthew 5:5).

Next, we must know God's Word so we can know what to pray for. God has personally given to me many promises from His Word in relation to my family, friends, and circumstances in my life. This knowledge released the faith to believe God for answered prayer. Jesus said, "If ye abide in Me, and My words abide in you, you shall ask what you will, and it shall be done unto you" (John 15:7).

Knowledge of His Word is closely linked with obedience to His Word. If we are abiding in Jesus, we are obeying. Abiding simply means living in Him, being so vitally related to Him that we will know what He wants.

If the previous concepts are true in our lives, then we only need ask in the name of Jesus for the things we desire and we will receive them (John 16:23-24). Just as the policeman comes and says, "Open up in the name of the law," and all the authority of the police force is behind him, so we can come in His authority. Thereby all the power and resources of God are at our disposal.

Finally, we all need a method of praying. The one I personally use is a Five Point Prayer Plan. This includes confession, praise, thanksgiving, intercession, and petition.

Confession – "If we confess our sins, He is faithful and just to forgive us our sins, and to cleanse us from all unrighteousness" (1 John 1:9). Our hearts must be clean; all sins confessed. God won't pay attention when we pray if we harbor sin in our lives. "If I regard iniquity in my heart, the Lord will not hear me" (Psalm 66:18). This is dealt with at length in the chapter, "The Making of a Wise Woman."

Praise and Thanksgiving – "Enter into His gates with thanksgiving, and into His courts with praise. Be thankful unto Him, and bless His name" (Psalm 100:4). It is impossible to separate these two kinds of prayer, but there is a difference. "Praise" is telling God how great He is and how much we love Him for who He is. "Thanksgiving" is simply saying, "Thank You" for all He has done for us. Psalm 116:17 says that we should offer to Him the sacrifice of thanksgiving. When we begin praising, we will continue thanking. When we are thankful, our hearts will burst forth in praise. Truly praise and thanksgiving are God's Siamese twins of prayer.

Intercession – "I exhort therefore, that, first of all, supplications, prayers, intercessions, and giving of thanks, be made for all men" (1 Timothy 2:1). One of the greatest ministries is praying for others. Jesus is our great example. He is seated at the right hand of His Father, interceding for us (see Hebrews 7:25). Anyone may participate in this ministry. Everyone should! Some feel especially called to this ministry.

Some are shut-in and bedridden, thinking their life is useless. The high calling of intercessory prayer is still open to them. A special notebook is helpful for this ministry. I recommend to you Peter Lord's *2959 Plan*. It has been a tremendous blessing to multitudes of lives, including my own.

Petition – "Give us this day our daily bread" (Matthew 6:11). Finally, we come to asking for ourselves. I have listed it last, on purpose. Nevertheless, we certainly should pray for ourselves many times a day. The real danger is that we might pray selfishly. If the rest of our prayer lives are in order, this part will be too. We won't always be praying "gimme" prayers. We will be praying, "Not my will, but Thine be done."

Solomon was given the privilege to ask God for anything he wanted. He prayed unselfishly. He asked for wisdom to judge his people. I want my chief prayer to be for me to be filled with the wisdom of God. If this is my desire, God has promised to answer my petition. "If any of you lack wisdom, let him ask of God, that giveth to all men liberally, and upbraideth not; and it shall be given him" (James 1:5).

BUILDING BRIDGES THROUGH OUTREACH

> And they that be wise shall shine as the brightness of the firmament; and they that turn many to righteousness as the stars forever and ever. (Daniel 12:3)

A woman should not isolate herself from others just because her priority is her home. Her primary field of outreach is indeed her home. However, she will reach out and touch those beyond her home. Even when children are small and time and energy are limited, there are creative ways of ministering to others and thus bringing joy to the world.

Even when at home you can reach out. For instance, the telephone can be a blessing or a curse. With it you can encourage and comfort, or you can gossip and tear down. You can even pray with someone on the phone. I have done it many times.

Cards and notes of comfort and cheer can be sent to the sick and bereaved. Don't forget to send a word to rejoice with those with new babies, a new promotion, or a special recognition.

As you step outside your door, you should walk into your neighborhood with the good news about Jesus. Start with a short friendly visit and a warm loaf of homemade bread or a pot of homemade soup, especially to greet newcomers on the block.

Some memorable occasions for me have been neighborhood Christmas parties centered around Christ. One year I had a ladies' neighborhood coffee. We had lovely Christmas goodies, sang Christmas carols, then I shared the true meaning of Christmas. Another time we had a family neigh-

borhood open house. We did the same thing except my
husband did the speaking. My children didn't think anyone
would come, but the whole house was full of men, women,
and children.

Neighborhood ministry get-togethers can be held any
time. Special days just provide a good "excuse" for doing it.
Why not try a "Love Thy Neighbor" coffee at Valentine's Day
or a "Celebrate the Wonder of Springtime" tea when the
flowers are in profusion. Or better yet, why not call your
neighbor on the phone right now and ask her to come over
for a hot cup of apple cider?

Witnessing "as you go" can be one of the most effective
ways of sharing Christ. Perhaps it will only be a smile to
start with, but you can be available. My friend, Barbara Ball,
said that she made a habit of just being "chatty for Jesus." If
you begin a friendly conversation, it may develop into an
occasion to share about Christ. If not, it didn't hurt to be
nice anyway. Life is much more exciting when anticipating
opportunities to minister for Christ.

I usually carry several different kinds of tracts in case I
want to give one to the bag carrier at the grocery store, the
service station attendant, or leave one with a tip at a restau-
rant.

Christian books are a wonderful means of encouragement and witness. There are hundreds of suitable paperback
books as well as others that will uniquely meet someone's
need.

Planned visitation is, of course, greatly used by the
Lord. In my lifetime I've visited in homes for the elderly, the
hospital, children's homes, jails, and in private residences.
As I go to share Christ, my purpose is to minister to others.
However, the joy that *I* receive is far greater.

Years ago when my house was filled with small children,
I bordered on feeling sorry for myself because I had so much
to do. During my Sunday School class visitation I knocked

on the door of a seventeen-year-old mother with a hydro-cephalic baby. Then I visited in a home for the elderly, and people were just sitting around with nothing to do. I still remember praising God all the way home for my household of healthy children and for so much work to do.

I have always been involved in my local church even before I was a preacher's wife. There are many opportunities to minister through the church. I have taught children, teenagers, and adults. I love them all. For years I have taught a class for children who are new Christians. They are such a joy. And just think, they have their whole lives to give in service for Jesus!

I've heard and studied about missions all my life. I have prayed for others who want to be missionaries and given my money so they could go. But one of the highlights of my life was when my husband and I went with a group of lay people from our church to Taiwan, the Republic of China, to share Christ.

What a blessing to experience for myself the oneness in Christ between us and the Chinese Christians there. It was so special that I really cannot explain exactly how I felt. We were only there for a week, but when we left I loved them so much. We went door to door witnessing with the Chinese Christians. In my own strength this type of witnessing is the hardest of all. But I felt *His* strength. When I listened to myself leading a Buddhist lady to Christ, it was hard to believe. How I praise God for this opportunity to bring the joy of Jesus to that part of the world.

I have helped plan evangelistic outreach projects for ladies through my church. Vonette Bright, the wife of Campus Crusade for Christ founder Bill Bright, helped me to envision how evangelistic luncheons are an effective means of sharing Christ. An outstanding Christian woman should be invited to speak about the difference Christ makes in a woman's world.

The ladies of the church are urged to invite a friend, neighbor, or acquaintance with a spiritual need. A creative theme is chosen, lovely decorations made, delicious food served, and beautiful music presented. All of this is pointed toward the time of sharing Christ. Of course, the occasion simply affords an opportunity to begin to continue a witnessing relationship with the one you brought to the luncheon.

Another women's outreach project that I have helped plan is a Christmas Home Tour. Our church has sponsored this event and there has been an excellent response each time. A few homes are chosen which are large enough for a group to get in and out easily. The ladies sign up ahead of time to begin the tour at different times so the houses won't be too crowded at one time.

Homes have been chosen which had different types of décor – Contemporary, Early American, Victorian, and so on. One home had braided rugs that the woman and her husband had made together as a hobby. Another lady had made her own lovely draperies. One home still had smaller children, showing a cleverly decorated playroom. Others were homes of those whose children were grown and showed more adult tastes. All of the homes were decorated for Christmas.

One year our theme was "Joy to the World." Each home was designated by a large painted plywood Christmas greeting in the front yard. Each home featured a different country of the world with hostesses dressed in native costumes and some decorations from that country. At the last home refreshments were served and a brief program given about the true meaning of Christmas. A few Christmas carols were sung, special music presented, and the pastor presented the message. A live manger scene with a man and wife dressed as Mary and Joseph was featured at the last house. Israel was the country featured.

CHAPTER EIGHT

WOMEN – MINISTERING UNDER AUTHORITY

There are two errors concerning women in the church. One is to say that she cannot say a word or serve in any capacity. The other is to say she can take any position of leadership – being equal with the man in authority

I take issue with the woman who suggested recently that the reason that some ministers don't feel led to ordain women to the ministry or elect them to significant places was that they were insecure and feared the loss of their leadership positions.

The fact is that the Bible teaches that women are not to take authority over men. All Scriptures on this subject must be studied comparatively and not just a couple of texts pulled out of context.

The Scripture in Galatians 3:28 which says, "There is neither male nor female; for ye are all one in Christ Jesus," has been used to justify women taking leadership roles over men. However, the same Paul who said, "There is neither male nor female...." also said in 1 Corinthians 11:3, "But I would have you know, that the head of every man is Christ; and the head of the woman is the man; and the head of Christ is God." Paul also wrote in 1 Timothy 2:11-12, "Let a woman quietly receive instruction with entire submissiveness. But I do not allow a woman to teach or exercise authority over a man, but to remain quiet" (NASB).

The passage in Galatians 3:28 does not refer to God's order of authority on earth. No – those who take this text as a proof-text for equal authority for women haven't studied the rest of the Scriptures that are related.

This passage in Galatians does teach that God loves the woman as much as the man. She has equal access to the throne of God. God doesn't consider her inferior, nor does He want the man to treat her so. This is a great liberation from the ideas of that day when the woman was considered no more than a piece of property. But it did not do away with God's order of authority. It only corrected an abuse of the woman's role.

It is true that Phillip's daughters were prophetesses (Acts 21:9), as was Anna (Luke 2:36). They could fulfill their roles with a meek and quiet spirit with all subjection (1 Peter 3:4).

There are several difficult passages concerning the woman's role in the church. One in 1 Corinthians 14:34-35 and one in 1 Timothy 2:11-13 says that the women are to keep silence in the church and if they will learn anything to ask their husbands at home.

If all related passages are studied carefully, one discovers that there were definite limitations placed on the woman's ministry in the public assembly. She was not permitted to be a teacher who would take authority over the man (1 Timothy 2:11-13). She was not to speak in tongues in the assembly (1 Corinthians14:34-35 – consider the entire passage which is 1 Corinthians 14:26-40), and she was not to challenge or question the male leadership in charge.

Kenneth Wuest in his Greek *Word Studies in the New Testament* says, "In the sphere of doctrinal disputes or

questions of interpretation, where authoritative pro-
nouncements are to be made, the woman is to keep
silence."[1]

It is obvious that the Scripture doesn't teach that a
woman can't say anything in the assembly, because Paul
says in 1 Corinthians 11:5 that a woman may pray or
prophesy in the church. However, there is a condition
attached to her ministry. She should have her head
covered. What the covering is has been debated through
the years. Whether it is some kind of headdress, long hair,
or hair long enough to look feminine and show the difference between male and female according to the custom of
the day (or whatever you believe it is), the significance of
the covering must be recognized. The purpose was to show
that the woman was in submission to God's order of
authority (under the man) when she spoke. "Therefore the
woman ought to have a symbol of authority on her
head..." (1 Corinthians 11:10, NASB).

The greatest damage being done today by women
taking the authority over men (and men allowing and
sometimes encouraging it) is that women are neglecting
their God-given chief assignment – which is to be:

> Teachers of good things, that they may teach the young women
> to be sober, to love their husbands, to love their children, to be
> discreet, chaste, keepers at home, good, obedient to their own
> husbands – that the Word of God be not blasphemed. (Titus
> 2:3-5)

Likewise, many younger women are neglecting the
spiritual instruction of their own children to lead in a
multitude of other projects.

Proverbs 31:10-31 clearly shows that a woman isn't a
"dumb bunny." Her abilities are varied and the scope of
her service is wide. She can be delegated much responsibility – but she lives "under authority." In this queenly

position she exercises much authority over those under her. But when she demands to be king – she loses her God-given power.

EPILOGUE

I'm looking forward to many more opportunities and years of witnessing for Christ. There is so much heartache and grief everywhere. I've discovered that what the world really needs is joy. The truly wise woman will commit herself to building bridges so she can share the joy of the world with those around her!

Joy to the World

THE WORLD NEEDS JOY!

The poor and hungry need this joy
        The red, and yellow,
                black, and white
The lonely and sorrowing
The defeated and dejected
The immoral and the moral
They all need joy!

THE WORLD IS LOOKING FOR JOY!

It looks here and there for joy
        It looks in possessions
                and in pleasures
        It looks in popularity
                and in power
But joy is never found in these!

I HAVE FOUND A JOY!

        A joy so deep within
        A joy that lingers
                even when I'm sad
                        and crying.

I WANT TO SHARE MY JOY!

> I want the world to
> know my joy
>> so —

JOY TO THE WORLD!

THE JOY OF THE WORLD CAME DOWN
THAT FIRST CHRISTMAS!

It came in a humble way
> Yet heralded by angels.
It came to a little town,
> The little town of
>> Bethlehem.

Hardly anyone knew that
> "Joy" came to the world
>> that night long ago,
But here I am almost 2000
> years hence –
>> And I know

I KNOW THE JOY OF THE WORLD!

Because one told one
> And two told two
>> And three told three
Then someone told me that

JESUS IS THAT JOY!

Born so long ago
Born to die upon a cross
Born
> To take my sadness
>> and my sin
> To take my loneliness
>> and guilt
> To take my fear and doubt
> To take my selfishness
>> and hate.

SO TO THE WORLD SO LONG AGO
THE FATHER SENT HIS
"GREATEST JOY"

The Joy that shared the
        Father's heart
The Joy in whom all fullness
        of the Godhead lived.

Jesus said,
        "Exchange your sadness
                and your weakness
                        for My Joy
                For My Joy shall be
                        your strength.
        I came to flood your life
                with Joy
        So full and overflowing
                that you too must
                        share my Joy
                                with those
                                        around
                                                you.

Around your family circle
Around the nearest block
Around the town in which you live
And then indeed
        Around the world."

NOTE

1. Kenneth Wuest, *Wuest's Word Studies* (Grand Rapids, Michigan: Wm. B. Eerdmans Publishing Co., 1956), p. 49.

Recommended Book List
For Balanced Christian Living

Books for Women

Bright, Vonette. *For Such a Time As This*. California: Campus Crusade for Christ, 1978.

Coble, Betty. *Woman: Aware and Choosing*. Nashville: Broadman Press, 1977.

Cooper, Darien. *You Can Be the Wife of a Happy Husband*. Illinois: Victor Books, 1979.

Dillow, Linda. *Creative Counterpart*. Nashville: Thomas Nelson, 1977.

Dobson, James. *Man to Man About Women*. Great Britain: Kingsway Publications, 1976.

Elliot, Elisabeth. *Let Me Be a Woman*. Illinois: Tyndale, 1976.

LaHaye, Beverly. *The Spirit-Controlled Woman*. Harvest House, 1979.

Ortland, Anne. *Disciplines of a Beautiful Woman*. Waco: Word, 1975.

Books on Home and Marriage

Brandt, Henry. *I Want My Marriage to Be Better*. Michigan: Zondervan, 1979.

Christenson, Larry. *The Christian Family*. Minnesota: Bethany Fellowship, 1970.

LaHaye, Tim and Beverly. *The Act of Marriage*. Michigan: Zondervan, 1976.

LaHaye, Tim and Beverly. *Spirit-Controlled Family Living*. New Jersey: Fleming Revell, 1978.

Martin, Dorothy. *Creative Family Worship*. Chicago: Moody Press, 1976.

Miller, Ella May. *A Woman in Her Home*. Chicago: Moody Press, 1968.

Miller, Ella May. *Happiness is Homemaking*. Virginia: Choice Books, 1974.

Renich, Jill. *To Have and to Hold*. Michigan: Zondervan, 1972.

Taylor, Jack. *One Home Under God*. Nashville: Broadman Press, 1974.

Wheat, Ed and Gaye. *Intended for Pleasure*. New Jersey: Fleming Revell, 1977.

Wright, Norman. *Communication, Key to Your Marriage*. California: Gospel Light Publications, 1974.

Books on Children

Brandt, Henry, and Phil Landrum. *I Want to Enjoy My Children*. Michigan: Zondervan, 1975.

Campbell, Ross. *How to Really Love Your Child*. Scripture Press Publications, 1977.

Dobson, James. *Hide or Seek, Self Esteem for the Child*. New Jersey: Fleming Revell, 1974.

Meier, Paul. *Christian Child-Rearing and Personality Development*. Michigan: Baker House, 1977.

Narramore, Bruce. *Help, I'm a Parent*. Michigan: Zondervan, 1972.

BOOKS ON CHRISTIAN LIVING

Adolph, Paul. *Release from Tension.* Chicago: Moody Press, 1956.

Baxter, J. Sidlow. *Going Deeper.* Michigan: Zondervan, 1959.

Billheimer. *Don't Waste Your Sorrows.* Pennsylvania: Christian Lit. Crusade.

Bounds, E. M. *Purpose in Prayer.* Chicago: Moody Press.

Chambers, Oswald. *Baffled to Fight Better.* Pennsylvania: Christian Literature Crusade.

Chambers, Oswald. *My Utmost for His Highest.* Pennsylvania: Christian Literature Crusade.

Chambers, Oswald. *The Moral Foundations of Life.* Pennsylvania: Christian Literature Crusade.

Fromke, Devern F. *Unto Full Stature.* Missouri: Sure Foundation, 1964.

Hession, Roy. *The Calvary Road.* Pennsylvania: Christian Literature Crusade, 1963.

Hession, Roy and Revel. *We Would See Jesus.* Pennsylvania: Christian Literature Crusade, 1950.

Huegel, F. J. *The Ministry of Intercession.* Minnesota: Bethany Fellowship, 1971.

LaHaye, Tim. *Spirit-Controlled Temperament.* Illinois: Tyndale House, 1956.

Nee, Watchman. *The Normal Christian Life.* Pennsylvania: Christian Literature Crusade, 1957.

Paxson, Ruth. *Life on the Highest Plane.* Chicago: Moody Press, 1928.

Taylor, Jack. *Prayer: Life's Limitless Reach.* Nashville: Broadman Press, 1977.

Taylor, Jack. *The Key to Triumphant Living.* Nashville: Broadman Press, 1971.

Thomas, Ian. *The Saving Life of Christ.* Michigan: Zondervan, 1961.

Torrey, R.A. *How to Pray.* Chicago: Moody Press

BOOKS ON NUTRITION

Baxter, J. Sidlow. *Our High Calling.* Michigan: Zondervan, 1967.

Elwood, Cathryn. *Feel Like A Million.* New York: Pocket Books, 1956.

Duffy, William. *Sugar Blues.* Denver: The Nutri-Books Corporation, 1975.

Josephson, Elmer. *God's Key to Health and Happiness.* Kansas: Bible Light Publications, 1962.

McGrath, William. *Bio-Nutronics.* New Jersey: Signet Books, 1972.

McMillen, S. I. *None of These Diseases.* New Jersey: Fleming Revell, 1963.

Nichols, Joe and James Presley. *"Please, Doctor, Do Something!"* Connecticut: Devin-Adair Co., 1972.

NATURAL FOODS COOKBOOKS

Albright, Nancy. *The Rodale Cookbook.* Pennsylvania: Rodale Press, 1973.

Ford, Marjorie Winn, et.al. *The Deaf Smith Country Cookbook.* Collier-Macmillan Publishers, 1973.

Lansky, Vicki. *The Taming of the C.A.N.D.Y. (Continuously Advertised Nutritionally Deficient Yummies) Monster.* Wayzata: Meadowbrook Press, 1978.

Martin, Faye. *Naturally Delicious Desserts and Snacks.* Pennsylvania: Rodale Press, 1978.